Enjoy the Journey.

How a nurse from West Virginia became known as "Mother Martha" in the East African country of Uganda.

Martha Hoy, RN

Author, speaker, and founder of Mother Martha Family Foundation.

Las Vegas, Nevada.

This book is dedicated to Dr. Viktor Frankl a man that not only survived what I would consider hell on Earth, the Nazi concentration camps, but thrived afterwards. He published 39 books and founded logotherapy, a school of psychotherapy which describes the search for a life's meaning as the central motivational force.

I am grateful for the lessons he taught and for his book, 'Man's Search for Meaning.'

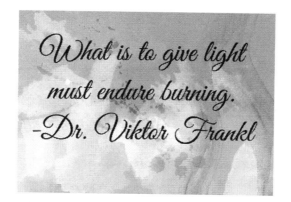

What is to give light must endure burning.
-Dr. Viktor Frankl

Contents

Introduction

"Only through unity do we have diversity and abundance. Each person a beautiful unique hue (hu-man) in the landscape of creation."

-Martha Hoy, RN

It is not what happens to you, it is about who you become. But along the way I enjoyed every moment of the journey of becoming who I was meant to be. I was a nurse in West Virginia in an abusive marriage. My life was saved by two young men who were orphans from Uganda. Then I became known as "Mother Martha" in Uganda.

Afterwards, I traveled the world. Sort of a way to "find myself" or "get my groove back." That I did, indeed. I built a new family during those travels. A family that includes people from all over the world. It was an amazing journey: I ate pizza in Milan, I dated an African Prince whose grandfather was the first president of Uganda and a king. I toured the palace that his grandfather the King had built. I saw the Eiffel Tower in Paris, I spent time in the Middle East, and I explored every inch of Las Vegas that a person could within two years.

Africa, especially Uganda, became my second home. I stood next to the source of the Nile

River in Jinja, Uganda, and explored all the beauty East Africa has to offer. Winston Churchill called Uganda "the pearl of Africa,' and I completely agree with him. My life's passion became to help the children of Bulamu Children's Village in Kampala, Uganda, where the two young men that helped me grew up.

Being a nurse helped me learn to connect with people as well in my travels. To connect with people no matter their culture, race, or economic status. There is something we have in common with another. We are all human beings, more alike than different. Most people go around pointing out our small differences, which causes separation between people. I hope you enjoy my story, that you learn something, or that it brightens you day.

Much love to you my friends,

Martha Hoy, RN

CHAPTER ONE:

The Catalyst That Changed My Perception.

Have you ever asked yourself, What the hell is wrong with people? I believe the root of that answer is simple: lack of love. Lack of love for self, and one another. That is the very root of it all. Every master that lived in the world such as Jesus, Buddha, and Mohammed told us to love each other as ourselves. People like Mother Teresa and the Dali Lama taught us love. However, human beings are not that simple. We like to complicate things. Let's face it, life can be messy and get really complicated at times. Especially in relationships, and especially when you start using the word love.

Each one of us is shaped by our life experiences. Who you are and who those around you are, right now in this moment, are shaped by their life's experiences. Each person with a different perception of everything built upon what they have lived through. No wonder life and relationships get complicated.

For example, have you ever taken an art class in which every person in the class is painting the same scenery or picture? The teacher stands in front of the class and says "Today we are going to paint a winter scene with a snowman; then gives instructions, step by step on how to do each brush stroke to create that masterpiece. At the end of the class each student shows their painting to everyone. Although each student was painting the same scene, each individual painting has its own unique touch. Different scarfs on the snowman, or they added a little cottage in the background. The same scene, but many different perspectives.

Perceptions we have of everything around us are built by our life's experience. Our cultures, religion, where we grow up, the people around us and the events that happen to us are all things that shape us. In knowing what has helped to shape another person we can have a greater understanding of each other. Understanding others creates more harmony within our relationships.

We should accept people for who they are, but never tolerate being treated in ways that leave us feeling disrespected or devalued. Of course, there is that all over the world, lack of compassion. I have seen it as a nurse - neglect, and abuse on all levels. Working in the emergency department, many times I have left my shift thinking, "I think I have seen every awful thing a person can do to another," Only to work a few more shifts to see something else that leaves me feeling sad and distraught.

Look at the intensions behind people's actions. If you truly observe people without judgment, people will show you who they are, and their intentions. I have seen people do the kindest of acts toward others for the wrong reasons. Usually to feed their ego, as if to say, "oh look at me, look at what I have done." I have seen someone hurt another's feelings or even physically hurt another, but not with the intent to hurt them. Intensions behind words and actions are important to consider within our relationships. Just as much as understanding and appreciating each other.

Everything is in the world, we live in duality: up and down, left and right, joys and sorrows, love and hate. However, what we choose to focus on will determine the quality of our lives. I stopped watching the news long ago. Watching the news daily will make you ask, "What in the hell is wrong with people?" I think of it this way, if it is something that I can do something about, then the information will make its way to me. You would not want someone to come into your home and dump their trash on your living room floor. Why allow them to dump their trash in your mind? I changed what I focused on daily, and so I changed my life.

My mentor used to say, life is like a bad camping trip. It is a temporary trip. Bad things can happen, like our tent falls, we do not catch our dinner, and there are bears out in the woods that scare us. But why can't we enjoy all the good things it has to offer? Like a beautiful sunset, the good company of those around us, and the beautiful flowers, for example. Pain is a part of life, but misery is a choice.

Have you ever just watched people, for example on the bus or the subway? Blank stares in their eyes; few people even laugh anymore. Listen to what others complain about or focus on? I feel as though so many people just exist and never truly LIVE. They spend their temporary trip focusing on all the negative and on what is wrong with what is going on around them, but never stop to really experience any of the good life has to offer.

My perception of the world changed on May 30, 2003. I was driving home from work on a Friday evening during five o'clock traffic. I was struck from behind at a high speed. Three people died, and I came out with multiple injuries. My life was changed in an instant. I was a young woman newly married, just starting my adult life. I was healthy and happy. Afterwards the only thing I could do was lie in bed, unable to move, and my only view of the world was the white tiled ceiling of my hospital room.

It was a catalyst that made me question everything. More importantly, it caused me to examine my own self. The white van in the picture above was the vehicle that struck me from behind. I was driving in the far-right hand lane, of a four-lane highway on my way home from work. During the day I was working at a bank, and at night I was attending West Virginia State University to obtain my nursing degree. It was a Friday evening; I had planned to take the weekend to get some rest. Next came a loud crashing sound and then total darkness.

I started drifting in and out of consciousness. The world around me was coming in and out of focus. I could hear voices clearly. During the moments of clarity, I became aware that I was in my car in the middle of the highway. The front of my car was facing the wrong direction and smashed into the concrete barrier in the middle. I could see a firefighter out of the driver's side window. As I was coming to, I could tell he was trying to get me out of my car. When I became completely aware of my body is when I became aware of the pain. It seemed to hurt everywhere, but the pain in my neck, knees and face were almost unbearable. I tried to turn my neck to look at the firefighter that was using some sort of tool to try open the door to get me out. Then I heard a voice say, "I need three body bags over here," and I drifted out of consciousness again.

My next memory was of coming out of the ambulance and into the trauma bay at the local hospital, in which my then-husband worked. A paramedic looked at me and said, "I think you will be fine but because of the severity of the accident, we just need to make sure everything is okay." Next came what I can only call "sensory overload." I was pushed into a room where many people surrounded my bed. They were asking me questions, shining lights in my eyes, and poking me with needles. An extreme rush of activity was all around me. I could not tell who in the room was asking me questions, but it was clear they were trying to figure out if I was oriented to the situation. They were asking questions like: who is the President of the United States, what day is it today, and what color is my shirt? It looked like a scene from Grey's Anatomy was happening around me, but I do not recall any McDreamy or Mc-Steamey at my bedside.

The trauma room had emptied quickly, but I had no concept of how long I had been in there. One nurse remained at my bedside. My sight was blurry so her face was just an outline, but I could hear her well enough. She came to me put her hand on my shoulder and said, "We are going to take you for a CT scan of your brain now. We think you are going to be fine, but we are just making sure. You have quite a bump on your head." I had not noticed the bump on my head because the pain in my knees and neck was overwhelming.

As I was coming out of the CT scanner, out of the corner of my eye I caught a glimpse of long dark hair, then I heard a man's voice say, "You are going to be moved to the trauma unit now." Then he turned to his co-workers that I could hear behind me, "That, my friends, is why you wear your seatbelt." I took that comment as a sign my injuries could have been worse.

I was settled in my hospital room, waiting for doctors to tell me what the damage was to my body, and a guess as to how long the recovery would take. Until the police came to my bedside, I had no idea what had even happened. I had just been trying to get home to a restful weekend. Now I was lying in a hospital bed in pain, and my only view of the world was the ceiling. A very sudden change in my perception of the world. The day of that car accident was a catalyst, one that would change my entire life.

Tim, my then-husband, was at my bedside, when a city detective came to take a statement from me. He introduced himself as Officer Jenkins with the Charleston City Police Department. He shook Tim's hand and then came to my bedside. I informed him that I could not physically give a written statement due to my injuries. He then pulled out a handheld audio recorder. "Then we will record your statement.

Mrs. Hoy what do you remember about this evening?" as he pushed the record button on the device.

"Not much." I said as tears began to run down my face. I could not wipe them away, so they were streaming down my face as I talked. "I was working at the bank, my boss told me that I had to stay a little longer to finish a project that was approaching deadline. I clocked out and was driving home as usual." Officer Jenkins asked, "Do you remember anything else?"

"I remember I was driving in the far-right hand lane of I-79, coming off the bridge where highway 79 splits off, you can turn left to go north or right to go south. Then just after the bridge, my world went dark and I heard squealing brakes. Then I was coming in and out of consciousness in my car as a firefighter was trying to get my door open." The tears then became more intense. "Then the next thing I remember is being here at the hospital."

After stating the date and time, Officer Jenkins thanked me for my statement and turned off the recorder. He put away his belongings, and turned to me, "Mrs. Hoy you were one of the lucky ones in this accident. Three people did not make it." That is when my mind flashed back to hearing the person say, "We need three body bags over here," when the firefighter was trying to get me out of my car. With the tears still flowing, I thanked the officer for his time. He shook Tim's hand as he left the room.

Tim walked forward to my bedside to comfort me. He was not a compassionate man, but was trying just at that moment. I told him I would be fine if he went home to get some rest. From then on, I was just waiting to hear what the trauma doctor's plan was for me. Tim reached down and kissed me on the forehead, said he would bring me a bag of personal care things tomorrow. After he left my hospital room, I pushed the nurse call bell and asked if someone could assist me to the restroom.

A slender young lady came to my bedside. She advised against me getting up out of bed this soon after the car accident. Stubbornly I insisted, so she reluctantly helped me get out of bed. As we were passing by the mirror above the sink in the restroom, I caught a glimpse of my reflection. My hair was full of blood and my face was unrecognizable. I began to touch my face as I looked in the mirror. I had no idea who the person was looking back at me. Most of the damage was on the left side of my face. The nurse must have realized my reaction, she said "Come on now, let's keep going," as if to say hurry up, let's not look in the mirror right now.

Not only had my ability to move been restricted, but I could not recognize myself when I looked in the mirror. Later I found out my face and head had hit the driver's door when I was struck from behind, leaving damage to the left side of my face. I had lost my identity. That is exactly what had happened. There is a saying,

"When you lose yourself, you find yourself." I do not want to admit this because I am not found of clichés, but that is what happened. My life as I knew it was over but losing everything led me to finding out who I am.

My recovery had begun, physical therapy started to work with me so that I could be strong enough to go home. Because of the impact from behind, my knees were smashed under the dashboard. Walking was painful and difficult, but I was doing it. When walking became easier and less painful, I could sit on a chair at the bedside to eat. I could see the faces of my nurses, the Jell-O on my plate and the view outside my window. When your life is reduced to only seeing a white tiled ceiling you appreciate everything much more when you can see the world around you once more. Something I told myself I would never take for granted again.

I recovered enough in a few days to go home. I was told by the trauma doctors that I needed multiple surgeries that included surgery on both knees and my face. The road to recovery was going to be long. I was working at the bank in the daytime and going to nursing school at night before the accident. I had wanted to be nurse since childhood. After my life was saved by all those wonderful nurses and doctors at the hospital, I was determined to finish what I had started. The positive side of stubbornness is when it is expressed as persistence.

CHAPTER 2:

The Recovery

The car accident was the catalyst that changed the course of my life. It is when I began to ask questions about everything that I had ever known, about people, and life itself.

As I sat in my bedroom recovering, I was getting bombarded with phone calls from friends and family wishing me well and asking me if they could do something to help me; some were just nosey, so they would have something to gossip about with each other. Susan, my friend and mentor called, "I am sending you a book." Not a surprise since she was an unconventional type of person. No well wishes from her, Susan was sending a book.

Everything can be taken from you in life, but how you choose to respond.

-Martha

A few days later a book arrived in the mail, 'Man's Search for Meaning', by Viktor Frankl. I was hesitant to read it, but my friend was reliable. There was no doubt she was wise. I made myself comfortable in my bed and began to read. I became so enthralled by this book I could not put it down. Hours went by before I knew it. It was daytime when I started reading that book and by the time I had finished it, I looked out the window to see that it was now dark outside.

Viktor Frankl was an Austrian neurologist and psychiatrist who survived Auschwitz concentration camp during World War II. He writes about what he observed during his time there. If anyone were to think about what a true "hell" on Earth might look like, I would say Auschwitz would be it. Everything was stripped away from people, their belongings, their families and even their names. Taking their names and giving them a number was not only taking away their identity, but taking anyway their humanness. Left with nothing but existence. Then given a uniform, forced into slave labor or into the gas chambers.

Dr. Frankl noticed that the people who smoked their last cigarette were losing their will to live and then would die shortly afterwards. Some people even chose to help those around them with what little they had. If not sent to the gas chambers during their stay, the people who chose how they responded, and who did not lose hope, who saw meaning in their lives, survived. Dr. Frankl not only survived but thrived after leaving Auschwitz. He wrote many books and went on to be the founder of logotherapy, a school of psychotherapy which describes a search for meaning as the central human motivational force.

There I sat with a look of amazement on my face. I looked down at what I had going on at that time. "This is all I have going on?" "Let's get on with it." I saw everything that I was going through in a different way. The biggest lesson that I learned from Dr. Frankl's story, is that everything can be taken from a person: their belongings, their families, and even their names. However, if we still have our lives, we have the one thing no one can take from us: how we choose to respond.

With a new perspective on life, I started to have the necessary surgeries beginning with my left knee. The home that Tim and I lived in was three stories. Going up and down stairs with two damaged knees was not easy. The left knee was where I hurt the most. My neck had improved and after a month I could take off the neck brace.

My home life was the same. The house I lived in I had built with Tim after we got married. We built it with our own two hands. An accomplishment I will always be proud of. Tim was not a compassionate man, but he has a great work ethic. Thankfully, we had finished building the house by the time I was in the car accident, because my body was no longer capable of that type of physical labor.

I always had my physical needs met, my medical bills were paid, we had a beautiful home, plenty of food on the table, and we had relativity nice things. Nevertheless, emotionally and mentally our home was not a healthy place. From the beginning of our relationship his family had nothing good to say to me or about me. I was just plain "not good enough" in their eyes. It was clear during my recovery he thought the same way. The verbal abuse I was living with caused me to feel bad about myself; I lived walking on eggshells every moment of my life. There I was, living in a toxic home recovering from my physical injuries from the car accident. I still could not recognize myself in the mirror. I had lost myself figuratively and literally.

In total I had 15 surgeries, including both knees and my face. Standing in the office of plastic surgeon Dr. Han Lee as he unwrapped my face just a few days after surgery, was a moment I will never forget. I waited six months for Dr. Lee to have the opening, for him to give me my face back. That he did.

He took the bandages off my face as I was looking in the mirror in his office. With every piece of gauze he pulled away, I began to see myself again. When he was done, I was me again. The image of the person I was before the evening of the accident. Tears started flowing down my face, but not tears of sorrow. Tears of pure joy.

I started walking from one side of our front porch to the other, each day taking a few more steps than I had the day before. Then I went to the mall with my crutches and walked from one side to the other. I was also determined to finish nursing school. It was a painful and long recovery process. However, I returned to nursing school. On May 4, 2005, less than two years after the date of the accident, I graduated with honors with a degree in nursing from the University of Charleston in Charleston, West Virginia.

A month after graduation, I started my first nursing job. Nursing is not an easy job: physically, mentally or emotionally. Once you see yourself as a victim of something then it can control you. I knew it would be more challenging for me because of the residual effects of the car accident, but I was determined to be the victor and not the victim.

Within my weakness lay my sleeping strength. I was forced to face myself in a metaphorical sense. I lost who I was, and my entire life was completely reset. For months I did not even recognize who I was in the mirror. While recovering, I spent a lot of time alone dealing with my physical limitations. Literally there was no running away from myself. I had to examine what had shaped me as a person and the perceptions I had of the world around me. Sometimes facing ourselves is the scariest thing we can do.

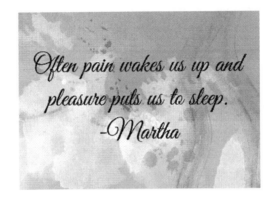

Often pain wakes us up and pleasure puts us to sleep.
-Martha

I do not claim to be an expert on relationships or marriage. Nevertheless, I have learned some things I would like to share. My relationship with myself had improved, and I was beginning a new career as a nurse. It felt like my life was renewed and I was more confident in myself. However, my marriage had not changed.

My then-husband was a good man in a lot of ways. I had everything I needed physically. We had a beautiful home that we had built together. We built it with our own hands. That is a test for any relationship. Five years of working side by side, trying to agree if a window or a door should go in a certain place. The relationship survived building our dream home. I feel as though the relationship began its decline after I started my first nursing job, and began to find out who I really was.

This book is not about that relationship or what happened in it. It was an important part of what shaped me as a person. The relationship lacked compassion. However, in the end, that was the experience that taught me more about love and compassion than any other experience in my life. When we are experiencing a lack of love, is when we appreciate love the most. I guess we could say that about most things. The lack of anything makes us appreciate it more when it comes around.

I am grateful for those who abused me, ignored me and bullied me. Because of those people and what they did, I came out stronger and wiser. Without them, I would not be the person I am today. Compared to who I was after the car accident until now. My previous self would not even recognize who I am today.

Abuse comes in different forms, physical, mental and emotional. For me it began with mental and emotional. Nothing I could do was right. I was the scapegoat for everything. I am sure I was blamed for all the wrong doings in the world at some point. My self-esteem was at its lowest point, I thought I was worthless, ugly and stupid. When you are told something repeatedly then you begin to believe it. I have found that people usually live up to the expectations that are put on them. The expectations put on me were low. I began to truly dislike myself because of the verbal abuse.

I was trying to understand why my marriage had become what it did. I questioned myself, the environment and many other things at first. Honestly, looking back now, the signs were there that he was abusive. I was just making allowances. Making excuses, such as he has a stressful job, or he was tired. Our lives were busy and many of the signs got ignored. The patterns were shaping but I was too focused on other things. Next thing I knew, I was living every moment walking on eggshells.

The dishwasher not loaded "properly" would trigger him. I stopped at an ATM once to withdraw money to buy lunch, but because I had stopped at an ATM that charged a 3-dollar fee it sent him into a rage of anger. My body was in constant fight or flight mode. Never being able to just be myself or to let down my guard. Not knowing what would set him off.

Most of what other people say and do is because of what is inside themselves. I learned this, because no matter how kind I was, how thoughtful I was, everything I did was wrong.

It would be nice if people came with warning labels, or holding signs. Like the comedian Bill Engvall says, "Here's your sign." Unfortunately, they do not, so we must notice how other people make us feel. Do not listen to what other people tell you, you should feel. Really stop, take a moment and notice how you feel around someone. How a person makes you feel says everything about them.

One person is not always wrong, we are getting something right daily. If you hear someone continuously blame others for their lives or misfortunes, that is just one red flag warning you might be dealing with a narcissist. Usually, they will blame the very person they are abusing. A narcissist will never apologize for anything, do not expect it because if you do you will be disappointed.

Control is the biggest warning sign. No one should tell you when to do things or how to do things. Trying to control what someone does with their personal belongings is a big warning sign of a narcissist. Love allows people to be who they are.

All emotions are rooted in either love or fear. Fear is from the ego and it needs to be in control. It is a trait of the human ego. Which is fine until it gets out of balance, and then that person begins to try to control everything around them as well as the people around them.

While everything was going well in my career, my personal life was falling apart. My health then began to follow. We tried to repair the relationship, but once a relationship is over, trying to mend it is like trying to plug a hole in the bottom of a sinking ship. You will just keep patching the hole, scooping out the water, until the entire ship sinks to the bottom anyway. If you feel in your heart a relationship is over, save yourself the work. Just say 'this ship has sailed.'

In 2015, I left the big house that we built together and moved into an apartment. It was my attempt to leave that relationship. I got unwanted advice such as "You married him, now you stick it out." Even my parents said such things to me. In November 2015, my parents said good-bye to me as a daughter as I sat in an empty apartment, crying on the floor after leaving my home and marriage. I got up off that floor and once again went back to the home we built together, again making an attempt to plug the hole in the bottom of the sinking ship.

November 2015 was a very dark period in my life. I was trying to repair a failing marriage. My family had pretty much disowned me. No one believed me when I cried out for help telling people what was going on in my life. I even reached out to co-workers and friends. I had started a new job at the medical center, but I knew it was not going to be a pleasant place to work when a fellow nurse literally "hissed" at me on the first day. My dog Coco that we had had for many years passed away of cancer. It appeared the ship was indeed sinking.

Chapter 3:

Along Came Geofrey

Then a light came to me in my darkness. Giving a purpose or meaning to my life. I met a young man, an orphan from Uganda, named Geofrey. Now I know most people's first reaction to that is, it must be a scam or some 90-Finance stuff. It was not. In fact, what happened next changed my life. Not only did it change my life, but it changed the lives of many other people.

During the summer of 2015 my friend Tracy, living outside of Minneapolis, adopted a young man named Ivan who grew up in Bulamu Children's Village in Kampala, Uganda. Geofrey had lost his parents, and I was in an abusive relationship. We filled a gap in each other's lives. I was the mother figure he was missing in his life. He was the kind, compassionate friend I needed in my life.

My father was an orphan, and growing up I could see the effects it had on him, not having a mother figure in his life. He had a daily routine of coming home from work every day to open the refrigerator to reach for a bottle of Miller Light. After we heard the refrigerator door closing, we never knew what the rest of the evening would hold for the rest of us in the home. When drunk, he frequently went straight on to saying how much he disliked women. My mother was usually the target of his fury. To this day, the smell of beer or cigarettes, especially Miller Light and Winston cigarettes, takes me back to those days.

After hearing him twist off the top of the Miller Light bottle we never knew what mood he would be in next. There were times when he was pleasant. But we never knew if he was going to start his verbal assault on my mother. Rarely did he hurt me or verbally abuse me, but I always felt the effects.

My father is the reason why I never turned Geofrey away. He was reaching out because he needed someone. Maybe if someone had been there to help guide my father, or just listen to him, that would have helped him. Never once did this young man ask for anything but a compassionate friend and guidance. I was a mentor in a way. We shared a passion for learning, so we began to have intellectual conversations about many subjects. Geofrey has a love for law and politics, and I have a love of science.

From the outside looking in we were completely different people. It seemed we should have nothing in common. Geofrey was a young African man, from a different economic status, different country, and different culture. I was a nurse from West Virginia, married, of a different economic status, a little older than him and, obviously, a white lady. I believe we are all more alike then different, people just go around pointing out those differences. Which causes separation between people. Within those small differences is where we can learn from each other.

We talked about our differences in lifestyles and cultures. Almost daily we engaged in talks about science, religion, psychology, philosophy, and politics. Politics being my least favorite subject, but Geofrey's favorite subject. We did not always agree, but we always learned from one another. We do not have to always agree into order to love one another. That was not just Geofrey and me, that is true for everyone on this planet.

Geofrey's friendship and support helped me get through not only the daily misery of an abusive relationship, but I had also been diagnosed with Multiple Sclerosis. MS is a disease of the central nervous system. Since every area of my life was in a state of dis-ease and my body and mind were constantly in fight or flight mode, it was not much of a surprise that my health began to fail. The first symptoms were numbness in my feet and legs especially after being on my feet at the hospital. At first I ignored the symptoms because of the chronic pain I had in both my knees and right hip after having surgery due to the car accident. Then something happened that forced me to stop ignoring the symptoms.

On New Year's Eve we were out with friends eating in a restaurant. I stood up to go to the bathroom, and suddenly I lost my eyesight, it was like I saw nothing but white, and then the world went dark. I had passed out on the floor on the way to the bathroom. That could not be ignored.

That led to months of tests, 4-hour trips to Cleveland Clinic, and around 15 visits to local doctors, before getting a diagnosis. The diagnosis came from a friend and co-worker, Dr. Stephen Lewis, a Cardiologist who I had known for years. I went to his office for an echocardiogram; right then and there he sat down next to me, looked me right in eye, and stated, "I think you have something called POTS. Postural Orthostatic Tachycardia Syndrome: when you stand up your heart rate increases, and your blood pressure decreases, which causes you to pass out when you stand up."

I trusted Steve, so I went through with the testing he recommended. After an MRI of the brain a couple of weeks later, I received a call to say that it was Multiple Sclerosis that was causing the POTS. I remember the day I was diagnosed well. After hanging up the phone, I thought I would have a pity party. Give myself 10 minutes to cry, scream, or throw things. After that I was going to choose to be the victor.

I am not saying it was easy. Being human is not easy for anyone. MS was another catalyst in my life that taught me many great lessons. After being on medication for a while, I could safely get up from a chair and walk without confirming gravity. Thankfully, I had Geofrey to help me through that time. My home life was no better. The sinking ship was slipping into the icy cold water even further.

Once again, I stabilized my health and went back to work as a nurse. Dealing with the injuries to my body from the car accident, residual damage from 15 surgeries, and now Multiple Sclerosis. That was what I was dealing with along with the abuse in my home. A state of dis-ease in all areas of my life, emotional, mental and physical. When we forget to care for one aspect of ourselves, then that causes disease throughout. All aspects of me were in a state of disarray.

Geofrey had helped me so much that I decided to pay for him to go to school. It was his dream to go to Law School and to someday be a politician. The problem he faced, just like the other orphans, was after leaving the orphanage they have no way to support themselves. No way to pay for college and no way to obtain job skills in order to support themselves. Helping Geofrey go to law school was a way to give a hand up and not a handout. A hand up so that he could continue to support himself and any future family. When I told him that I had decided to help him go to school, I said the only thing I asked for in return was that he pays it forward in some way. To be kind to someone else in some way -it did not have to be anything big, just one kind act.

Uganda on average has 2.5 million orphans in a country of about 40 million people. Those numbers alone just make my head spin. What is the cause? Several factors, including poor leadership, the HIV/AIDS epidemic, separated refugees from other countries, etc.

When I say orphans, I mean homeless children living in the streets by themselves. If they are lucky enough to find a way into an orphanage, then once they age out of the orphanage, they have no way of supporting themselves as adults. I could not solve this problem, but I could start by helping just one young person, Geofrey. Asking him to pay the kindness forward was a good way for the solution to spread out and affect others in a positive way. By setting the focus on the solution, not the problem, beginning by giving one person a hand up.

Geofrey graduated in December 2017, and at that time I was in Washington DC. It was Christmas time, all the states of the union had beautiful trees up around the nation's capital. I love visiting the US historical sites on Capitol Hill. I have been very blessed to see the United States Constitution in person many times, the White House, the Capitol Building, and the Washington Monument. I have stood where President Lincoln was shot and where he died. I have a cousin, Jerry, who is buried in Arlington National cemetery, and I pay my respects at his gravesite during each visit.

The President at that time, Donald Trump, was signing a bill into law that would help people with Multiple Sclerosis get access to medication. A subject I am passionate about. Most people with MS cannot afford to get care, because the disease modifying drugs for MS cost on average 55,000 dollars yearly. At that time I was fortune enough to have great health insurance and access to medication, when many around the country did not.

During that trip something happened that changed the course of my life, as Tim and I were walking around the Reflecting Pool in front of the United States Capitol building. It was evening, and it had begun to snow. There were a few secret service agents nearby, but it was mostly quiet. It was a romantic scene and a great time for a beautiful walk back to the hotel.

That quiet, romantic scene did not last long. Moments later I knew it was time to leave this relationship. As I said before, this book is not about him or what he did to me. But at that moment, what he did and said caused me to end up walking back to the hotel by myself, crying and stating out loud to myself, "How could I have not seen this, he does not even like me." I knew then it was imperative that I leave this marriage.

It was an awkward flight back to West Virginia. Knowing that I was flying home just to be next to my biggest enemy. When I got home and settled, I got a phone call from Geofrey. He called to say that he and some friends had figured out how he was going to pay it forward. They took up donations, rented a truck, and went into Bidi Bidi. Bidi Bidi at that time, December 2017, was the largest refugee camp in the world. People were fleeing South Sudan, going into northern Uganda due to civil war. The camp had grown to over 270,000 people. Geofrey began to send me pictures from his trip. With each picture that came through in a text, tears began to roll down my face. The pictures of the children of Bidi Bidi impacted me the most. But then I fell to my knees in joyful tears.

Geofrey had gone on to explain that it felt so good to help others and his friends, that he decided to start a charitable foundation in Uganda. AMKA Foundation Africa in Kampala,

Uganda, an organization to help young people coming out of the orphanages obtain job skills. Never did I think when I started my friendship with Geofrey that we would end up impacting the lives so many people in a positive way. Opening my heart to Geofrey changed his life and the lives of others, but it began to change mine as well.

From December 2017 to May 2018, I began to break down my marriage on paper. We had sold the house that we built together. I began to give some things away, and sell others. One day when I was cleaning my bedroom, I got the feeling I should pack a suitcase. So I packed a white suitcase and put it in my closet at the foot of my bed.

> Not all catalyst come in the form of a nice person. Often pain wakes us up and pleasure puts us to sleep.
> –Martha

CHAPTER 4:

She Left With Just A Suitcase
And Never Looked Back

On May 13, 2018 - Mother's Day - which is ironic since Geofrey and his friends had called me 'Mother Martha' in Uganda since 2014, just like the day of the car accident my life was changed in an instant. Sometimes I think God or the Universe, whatever label you feel comfortable with, has too much faith in my strength. However, I had been trying to plug the hole in the bottom of that sinking ship for too long. That relation-ship was bound to go suddenly crashing into the icy waters. On that day, it certainly did. I had to leave my home suddenly, with just a single suitcase - the suitcase that I had packed in my closet.

I was lying in my bed, watching TV, wearing my pajamas, with my dog at my side. Then suddenly my then-husband Tim entered the room. I knew from the way he approached me that if I did not run, I would not survive this interaction.

Look around you right now. If you had to leave with just a suitcase, walking away from everything you ever knew and had, where would you go? How would you survive? At that very moment I understood how the refugees at Bidi Bidi must have felt when they had to leave their homes so suddenly.

I had no-one to turn to, and nowhere to go. My friends and family had turned away from me. Despite the fact I had reached out to them many times. That included co-workers, long time friends, my parents, and neighbors. A re-altor that I had a long-time business relation-ship with was the only person that responded to me, she had looked at me in my kitchen just a few months before and said, "Martha do you need to leave with me right now?" I did need to, she was correct, but things played out in a much different way.

Now this book is not about my then-husband and what he did on that day or any other day. Narcissists think everything is about them. This book is about the lessons I learned from my story, not about him.

As I said, I was lying in my bed watching tele-vision with my dog when he entered the room. I knew from the way he came at me that it was going to become violent. As he reached for me, I fought to roll out of the bed. I grabbed the suitcase from my closet. There was a strug-gle down the hallway. He was screaming at me, "You will never amount to anything, no one else will ever put up with you." Words I was used to hearing daily. The struggle contin-ued down the hallway and out the front door.

I rolled that suitcase to the end of the front porch while fighting him off. At the top step just before the driveway I stopped, looked him right in the eye and said, "You will never see my face again!" Tears running down my face, I turned to put that suitcase in the back seat of my car, got in and began driving. I had no idea where on Earth I was going to go. I was a mess, I was afraid, with tears flowing down my face. I had no one I could turn to, but there was one person I knew I could trust. Geofrey.

Geofrey, the orphan in Uganda. He had proven to me that he had my back for the past four years, despite the fact that he was 7,000 miles away. I began to drive north on I-79. Once I was at a safe distance away from the house, I pulled over at a rest area. I made two phone calls, the first to Geofrey to tell him what had happened. He immediately said, "Go to Minnesota to my brother's apartment. He will keep you safe." Ivan was his brother, who my friend Tracy had adopted from Bulamu Children's Village in Uganda and brought to the United States in 2015. At that point I had two options, return to my home knowing that death was the most probable outcome, or I could fly from West Virginia to Minnesota to stay with someone I had never met and had only ever seen in pictures. Nevertheless, going back was not an option I was willing to take.

The second phone call was to Ivan in Minnesota. I told him what had happened just an hour earlier. He agreed to allow me to come stay with him, no questions asked. Ivan said, "Because of everything you have done for my brother you can come here." I hung up the phone, stopped to get gas, then began to try to figure out how I was going to get to Minnesota. After I was done pumping gas into my car, I called my friend Barb.

Barb and I had been friends since high school. She still lived in our hometown of Fairmont, West Virginia, which was just a two-hour drive from where I had been living in Charleston for the past decade. She was the single mother of one daughter. Her daughter had gone off to college the previous fall, and Barb was in a career transition. Fairmont is a small town, the only things it is known for are pepperoni rolls and being the hometown of Mary Lou Retton, the gymnast who won a gold medal in the 1984 Summer Olympics. At that time, Barb was packing to move to Las Vegas, Nevada, quite a change from our small home town.

I arrived at Barb's front door around nine o'clock that evening, still in my pajamas. My eyes red and swollen from crying and my hair a mess. Barb answered the door looking about the same, disheveled hair, wearing sweatpants and a big T-shirt. She was around 35 years old, with blonde medium length hair and a round face. We were always opposites in our appearance. In high school I was thin, with long brown hair and a long-boned face. We both looked a bit different now some years later, but I like to think we both aged well.

Barb opened the door, "Well get in here. Are you hungry?" "No," I replied, as I carried my suitcase through the doorway. I took my suitcase to her spare bedroom that was her daughter's room. Her daughter had gone away to college the fall of the previous year, so it was mine for a few days. We both sat down in her living room after I put my things away. "Tell me what happened? You look like hell." Barb was never one to hold anything back. She is a straight shooter that curses like a sailor, but she has a good heart.

As I recounted what had happened just a few hours before, I did not cry. I think I had run out of tears at that point. "What are your plans now?" Barb asked, with a look of concern her face. "I am going to Minnesota to stay with Ivan, Geofrey's brother." That statement turned her look of concern to one of shock. "Well alright then. You can stay here for three days and help me pack up my things for my move to Las Vegas. I am going to bed now. Help yourself to whatever is in the kitchen." She went into her bedroom and closed the door.

That left me there, alone on the couch, to process what had just transpired in the last 8 hours of my life. As I relived what had just happened, I realized I had now left everything I had ever known; my entire life was reduced to a suitcase.

Staying safe was the most important thing at that moment. I knew I had to put a large distance between me and the past. I booked my flight to Minneapolis/Saint Paul Airport three days hence from my phone as I sat there on the couch. I thought to myself that it was time to put a whole lot of miles and a whole lot of Jesus between me and that place.

We spent three days doing the things we did as teenagers, such as talking about boys, eating pizza, and drinking coca-colas. I helped her pack her belongings for her move across country. I was pulling a lot of sweatpants and sweatshirts out of her closet. I stated, "Barb, you need update your wardrobe. You are moving to Las Vegas, darling"."

Barb replied with a scowl on her face, "I have been a single mother for 10 years Martha, leave me alone."

"Barb, well now your daughter is in college and you will be living in Las Vegas, it's time for a redo of this closet. We will have to have a funeral for your lady parts if you don't."

We both laughed at my ridiculous joke.

Barb took a piece of pizza out the box to eat, "Fine, I will get rid of a couple pairs of these sweatpants."

I grabbed a pair of sweatpants with holes in them and threw them at her, "Here, start with these."

After a few days in my hometown, pretending to be teenagers again, I set off for Chuck Yeager

Airport just two miles south back in the town I had just run from, Charleston, West Virginia. I got ready that morning and Barb walked me to the front door. "Call me when you get to Ivan's place." Barb said to me in a motherly tone.
"I will call you as soon I get settled."
Then we hugged each other in the doorway, not knowing when we would see each other again.

I made a stop along the way, at my attorney's office to file for divorce. I sat at the end of a long wooden table waiting for my attorney to come in with the papers I needed to sign. She walked in the room with a stack of paperwork and laid it on the table in front of me. Then looked at me and stated, "You cannot leave the state of West Virginia with your car, it is marital property, the judge will not allow it."
I replied, "Fine, but before I allow him to kill me, I will put a brick on the gas pedal and push that car into the Kanawha River." I then pointed out of the window of her office to the view of Kanawha River. The fact that a car is more important than a person's life should make everyone think carefully before marrying anyone.

I signed the necessary papers to file for divorce, then I drove that car to the parking garage of the airport, texted my attorney the number of the parking spot it was parked in, and told her I would FedEx the keys when I landed at my destination. I was boarding a plane to my freedom. Cars can be replaced; people cannot be replaced.

Minneapolis-Saint Paul International Airport was my destination. Some place I had never even visited, to live with people I had never met. Some might say that was courageous. I guess looking back I believe it was. But it was necessary. I left behind everything I had and ever knew. Turning back was not an option.

That flight out of Charleston, West Virginia on that day in May, felt like pure freedom. Like I was ascending out of hell. As much as I tried to understand why those around me were treating me the way that they were, a flower just cannot bloom in toxic soil. We should accept everyone for who they are, but we should never tolerate being treated in ways that leave us feeling disrespected or devalued. That flight was the beginning of my new life.

When I arrived at Minneapolis/Saint Paul Airport I found a place to sit down, so I could tell Ivan where he could find me. There I sat in the airport waiting for a young man to pick me up that I had never met. All I had was a picture of him on my phone, a stranger that I was going to live with and trust that he was going to protect me. I texted him, "I am sitting next to the black grand piano," along with a picture of the piano. I sat on the bench looking around, and then looking at my phone, at the face in the photo. A tall, slender, young African man with big, beautiful eyes and a killer smile came around the corner a few minutes later. That smile looked just like Geofrey's smile. I knew instantly that it was Ivan. A sense of relief filled my body at the sight of his smiling face.

We hugged each other, and he said "I cannot believe you are here." We walked in silence to his car and he loaded up my suitcase. He said, "I wish I had a better car to pick you up in." I replied, "Darlin', I am just grateful you are helping me. What is next?" I meant like in 'what is for dinner', but he thought I was contemplating life. He said, "Now we live."

Looking back now I guess that was a simple yet profound statement. It was time for me to live. Truly live my life. I could heal and find out who I am, without all the noise from those who had been around me previously. Sometimes in life we just exist. I had done plenty of that. Now it was time to live.

It reminded me of something my mentor used to say, "Life is a like a bad camping trip. It is a temporary trip. Bad things happen such as bugs biting you, you do not catch your dinner, there are bears in the woods that scare us, your tent may fall, but why can't we enjoy all the good things as well. The beautiful sunset, the flowers and the good company of those around us. Pain in life is inevitable, but misery is a choice." Her words of wisdom went through my head as I was seeing the town of Minneapolis for the first time.

I looked out the windows of Ivan's car as we were driving through the streets of Minneapolis. After losing the ability to see the world around me after the car accident, I never again underestimated the ability to take in the sites, sounds, and smells of the world around me. We arrived at Ivan's third floor apartment in Blaine, Minnesota in the late afternoon. As we opened the door, his roommate Joe was there to greet me. It was comforting to see another smiling face. He introduced himself and told me to make myself at home. Joe was the definition of tall, dark and handsome, with broad shoulders, wide facial features, a muscular body, and a warm smile. I felt immediately safe as I walked through the front door.

Ivan had cleared out his bedroom for me a couple of days before I arrived. He directed me to his room, and said that I could settle there. I unpacked my things while Ivan made up the couch for himself. We ate dinner together that evening. Conversation was the usual "getting to know you" stuff. What do you do for a living, where did you grow up? That type of conversation. That night as I lay in the bed of a stranger, in a town I had never been in before, I felt of sense of calm. Calm because I was safe. I never had to go back to that life in West Virginia again.

I ended up spending the next four months with Joe and Ivan in Blaine, Minnesota. It is not the most exciting place to live, there's not much there but a Wal-Mart, an ice skating rink and a Dairy Queen. Blaine is not far from Minneapolis and Saint Paul, the twin cities. Not sure why they are called that, because the two cities seem completely different to me. Saint Paul is a town with its roots deep in the Catholic religion. It has old temples and beautiful Roman style architecture. Minneapolis is more modern with tall buildings and skyscrapers. It was a great place to heal. You never know how toxic a situation really is, until you are out of it. It was like I was breathing fresh air for the first time in a long time. Healing is messy and takes time. Looking back now I wish I would have been more patient with myself.

No one from my home or my family even tried to find me. I just walked away from my life and not one person bothered to try to find out what had happened to me. Not even my parents. No matter how good a person you are, there are people that will never support you. Even those you think should support you, or those that society thinks should support you. It was hurtful. I kept thinking, "How could a mother or father not care about what happens to their child?" I had gone to my mother repeatedly to tell her what was going on. She had just told me to stick it out.

Not only had I begun to heal, but I began to build a new family. Everything I ever had, or had been, I left in West Virginia. However, with those things gone, now there was room for things rooted in love. All that I had from the past, besides that old suitcase, were the lessons I learned. I wanted to share what I had learned from my experiences with others. That is when I started writing the book 'Lead with your Heart.'

Getting used to single life again and living with two single young African men from such different cultures was a big change, but a welcome change. We learned a lot about each other. Ivan cooked Ugandan food for us. Joe and Ivan argued about whose country had the most gorillas, Uganda or Rwanda. I am from West Virginia, a state located in the south east United States, so all their conversations were educational to me.

I love food and I fell in love with the food from both cultures. We had conversations about the things they had seen and experienced since coming to live in the United States. It is educational to see your own culture from the perception of those who are from other places in the world. I found myself saying, "I am not sure why we do things that way?" I learned a lot about myself, as well as their cultures and beliefs.

Joe is a very social guy. Frequently going out with friends, or friends coming over to visit. Ivan is a quiet guy, who would rather stay at home, watch movies and write music. I used to say it would take a threat from the North Korean government to get him out of that apartment to go anywhere but work. Both young men were supportive and respectful. Frequently calling me Momma Martha which made me giggle, because I am not that much older than Joe. Nevertheless, I understood it came from a place of respect for me.

I never got involved in politics in my life, although that was Geofrey's favorite subject. I just feel that I can think for myself. I am liberal on some subjects yet conservative on others. However, I somehow found myself getting involved in politics unintentionally. I was watching television one evening, siting on the living room couch with Ivan. I was writing but glancing up at the television periodically. I looked up to see violence on the screen. It was a group of men beating up men and women in what looked like the inside of a government building. Suddenly I forgot about writing and began to watch what was happening on the television screen. It was so barbaric and violent. I looked over at Ivan and said, "This is the government in Uganda?" with a mixed look of disgust and surprise on my face. Ivan looked over at me and stated, "Unfortunately, that is the parliament in Uganda."

I knew little about the political history of the country. I knew they had been suppressed by a dictatorship for the past 33 years. I knew a few stories about Milton Obote, the former Prime Minister, and the bloody history of former President Idi Amin. On the screen, I saw a man get hit in the head with a chair. I shouted out in shock, "OH MY! That poor man." That man was Zaake Francis Butebi, a Ugandan member of parliament. He and I would end up becoming friends shortly after I saw him being physically assaulted on television that day, in the summer of 2018. Seeing that footage of how brutal the government was on the floor of parliament gave great insight into the state of the country.

I got a job as nurse at an Assisted Living Facility in Saint Paul, Minnesota, called Gracewood Senior Living. The commute to my job in the mornings was a great time to take in the beauty of the twin cities. During my commute, I got to watch a 150-year-old temple be restored. The quiet time in my car all alone, coupled with the beautiful scenery, was helpful to me. The scars from the trauma of living in a constant state of dis-ease, physical, mental and emotional, were beginning to heal. My physical scars healed right away, the emotional and mental ones would take a while longer.

The ladies working at Gracewood Senior Living were so good to me. A welcome change from the bullying I had experienced back in West Virginia at the medical center. During lunch time the cook would bring me a plate of food while I was working at the computer in the nurse's office. It was like a little family. I was being supported and loved at home and at work for the first time in my life. Which helped greatly toward my healing.

Some people have told me they think how I got my divorce was badass. On July 7, 2108, I clocked out for lunch at my job, went to my car and called my attorney on her cell phone. I had refused to return to the state of West Virginia because it still felt it was unsafe to return there. My attorney had also expressed feeling unsafe when my then-husband would show up at her office, so getting permission from the judge to not physically attend the divorce hearing, but to do it over the phone was granted. I remember hearing the judge's pen gliding across the paper over the phone as he signed his name on the divorce papers. I said, "Sir you have no idea how you changed the world by signing those papers." Now I am not sure why that came out of my mouth at that moment, but it was just a feeling I had. Not sure if I would say it was the most badass thing I did during my journey, but it was certainly necessary for my safety.

CHAPTER 5:

Viva Las Vegas

After four months with Joe and Ivan, I decided it was time to move on with my life. I had healed enough to leave the safety of their apartment. My divorce was final, and I thought I was much safer than before. By October 2018, I was on a plane to Las Vegas, Nevada. I now make the joke that I moved from the most boring place on the planet, Blaine Minnesota, to the most exciting place on the planet, Las Vegas. However, I am incredibly grateful for my time in Minnesota and the family that I began to create there. Nevertheless, it was time to move on to start a new life. I had healed enough to begin my life as a newly single lady.

Las Vegas is a place known for its bright lights, and fun. It is known as Disneyland for adults. I do not drink or gamble, but I knew Vegas had much more to offer me than those things. My friend Barb, who I had spent a girls' weekend with just four months earlier in West Virginia, was already settled in Las Vegas. We were talking on the phone one evening when she just said out of nowhere, "Hey, move to Vegas; we can be two single ladies living off the Vegas strip, restarting our lives."

I received little of my personal belongings that I had accumulated in all those years of my marriage. But it did not matter in the big picture of things. I had left with just a suitcase, leaving him with what mattered to him the most, material things. To me things can be replaced, people are more important. If you do not take care of a person's heart, then all you are left with is a paper trial and a house full of stuff.

Just like when I had arrived four months earlier, I was sitting on that bench in the Minneapolis-Saint Paul International Airport next to the black grand piano with my suitcase. Four months earlier when I was sitting on that bench, I was beaten down, abused and a shell of a person. This time I was much more healed, and now it was time to rediscover who I was. Self-discovery is an important part of our success. When caterpillar researchers help butterflies to escape their cocoons, it results in misshapen wings. This time was the beginning of me discovering who I was meant to be, for myself.

It was the beginning of a new life. I was not afraid; turning back was never an option. I knew what was ahead of me was better than what had been. I was strong and wise enough to take care of myself. This caterpillar was beginning to break out of its cocoon.

Driving down Las Vegas Boulevard for the first time, seeing the bright lights and the crowds of people on the sidewalks with the song Viva Las Vegas playing in my car was so exiting. My future was an open book with blank pages. A blank canvas in which I could paint whatever picture I wanted. With each word or brush stroke I could determine what my life was going to look like.

I had been through so much trauma. Domestic abuse, my friends and family had turned their backs on me and rejected me. I still had residual effects from the 15 surgeries due to the car accident, and I was living with Multiple Sclerosis. However, all of that was now in the rear-view mirror. I had learned to adjust to my physical ailments. My life may had been reduced to just a suitcase full of personal effects, but I still had my life. Now I was free to make my life look like whatever I wanted it to look like.

I had the one thing no one could take from me, the right to choose how I responded to what had happened to me. I was ready to take everything that had happened and turn it into something rooted in love.

This was the time to find out who I was. People had told me who I was for years. Told me how I should think, feel, and what I should do. Especially when you are in an abusive situation in your home, your every move is criticized and controlled.

The perceptions that others have of you should never define you. Do not doubt yourself, just be you. A person's value does not decrease based on the inability of others to see it. Now everything from the past that had been making me unhappy was gone. Now there was room for people who could see my worth, and room for new things rooted in love.

Our lives are like the journey of a train, the trip has a beginning and an end. People will come into your life as passengers, each one getting on and off at different stops along the way. Each person that comes into your life, no matter how long they stay on the train, teaches you. Sometimes the only thing they teach you is how not to be. Others will come into your life, who love you. Everyone has their own traumas and issues from life. Do not be quick to push away someone that might love you just because they do not present themselves in a way that you thought, or even society says, they should. Love comes in many forms. We should never push away love or a meaningful relationship just because it does not come in a certain way. We love our friends in a different way then we love our siblings, or children. Geofrey and I love each other in the way a mother loves her son, or a mentor/mentee relationship. If I had pushed Geofrey away, then who would have been there when I needed someone the most?

When you open your heart to another, it not only changes their life it changes yours too. -Martha

Just four months earlier Barb and I were packing up her apartment in Fairmont, West Virginia to move to Las Vegas. Now I was in Las Vegas unpacking the few belongings I had into her apartment. The goal was to be two single ladies living close to the Las Vegas strip, restarting out lives. We had been friends for a long time, and I had shared in the joy when Barb's daughter was born. Barb celebrated with me when I got married. Moving in together made sense. We were both at a point in our lives that was sort of a redo, and we had been friends most of our lives.

When I moved in with her in Las Vegas, I had no idea that she would leave my life in the way that she did. She had voiced that she did not like Vegas during the four months that she was there while I was in Minnesota. I thought she would like it better once I was with her, doing things together. She had complained about West Virginia, and now she was complaining about Las Vegas. Some people are just about as happy as they make up their minds to be.

Barb frequently compared Nevada to West Virginia, complaining about the things she did not like. The things I like about Nevada were the things that were different than West Virginia. The weather of the desert is dry. In the summer it is extremely hot, so there is little greenery. I began to call the rocks on the side of the road, Nevada grass. West Virginia is lush, with green trees and grass in the summer. In the wintertime in West Virginia the leaves fall off the trees to make room for winter snows. I was excited about my new environment, so there were no complaints from me.

I found a job as a nurse in a nearby hospital shortly after I got settled into the apartment. I began to explore Las Vegas on my days off from the hospital. One of the things that I found I loved about the area, is that there is always something to do. If you like the outdoors, it is a short drive out of Las Vegas to places like Mount Charleston, the Hoover Dam, or Lake Mead in Boulder City, Nevada. The Las Vegas Boulevard has the bright lights, the iconic casinos and live entertainment. It has everything you could possibly want within a short distance. Unlike Barb, I was beginning to thrive in my new environment.

Three months after moving into the apartment, I was coming through the door after a long shift at work. I went to put my keys on the stand near the front door. Instead of landing on the stand, the keys fell to the floor. I looked down to see the stand was gone. As I looked around, I noticed the apartment was completely dark. As I turned the lights on in each room, I did not see any sign of a struggle or signs of something wrong. In fact, I saw nothing.

There was only the couch left in the living room; my bed was still in my bedroom and my clothes in my closet. I slowly opened Barb's bedroom door, but her room was empty. The apartment was empty, and Barb was not there. Many things started going through my mind. There was no note to be found as to her whereabouts. My phone had not rung and there was no text message from her. I thought maybe I should call the police.

Frustrated, I sat down on the couch to collect my thoughts. Then I received a text: "I went back to the east coast to be with my daughter. You had better take my name off that Foundation. I am not helping anyone, especially people I don't know."

Before moving to Las Vegas, Barb had agreed to help me start a charitable foundation for children in Las Vegas. One that would benefit children in the United States and in Uganda. The Mother Martha Family Foundation had been established in Las Vegas just a couple a weeks before. I remembered that she had told me that she was worried about her daughter back in West Virginia. People do and say the things they do, because of what is inside themselves. She had her reasons for doing what she did. Nevertheless, It did not make sense to me as to why she would leave without any notice.

There I sat, on the couch in an empty room, thousands of miles away from anyone I knew. I felt betrayed and alone. Barb was the only person that was still in my life from West Virginia. She had paid $25.00 in bills in the 3 months we lived together. She did not help me with establishing the charitable foundation. I had known Geofrey for four years, he was 7,000 miles away in an East African country, but he was there for me when I needed someone. He, along with his brother and Joe, helped me no questions asked. Barb whom I had known for years, living close to me, had not kept her promise and left me thousands of miles away from home alone in an empty apartment. No note, no explanations as to why, just a text message.

Of the people who had been physically close to me, many, not all, mistreated me, ignored me and some abused me. But the people who were physically the furthest away from me always had my back. Communication is the exchange of information, but connection is the exchange of emotions. This is why we can feel lonely in a crowded room, yet feel a connection with someone far away.

People had always told me who I was, how I should feel and what I should do. Especially when I was living in the toxic environment of domestic abuse. However, if I had listened to others and lived my life the way everyone told me to live my life, I may not have been still on Earth past May 13, 2018. I learned to drown out the voices of others and listen to my own inner voice. I learned to ask myself, how does this choice make me feel? How does this person make me feel? Chances are, if a person or situation makes you feel uncomfortable then it is not for you. If a situation or person makes you happy then it is probably right for you. Discernment over judgment. Being discerning means to know when something is not right for you, yet not judging, belittling or devaluing them. I had learned to drown out the voices of others, and I learned to lead with my own heart.

There I sat in an empty room with what was left of my life. I was thousands of miles away from anyone I knew. Once again, I was forced to face myself. To look within myself at how

I felt and who I was. Facing our traumas, our joys, our hurts, our downfalls, and our beauty. Facing ourselves can be one of the most courageous and difficult things we can do.

As I looked back at what had happened in just the past year of my life, a lot of things had taken place in a short period of time. I had lived in an abusive home, my health was falling apart, but I did a very courageous thing by just walking out with only a suitcase, without knowing where I was going to go. Just a few months before I had no one, and nowhere to go. Now I had Joe and Ivan as a part of my family. I knew I could take care of myself. I was no longer that abused woman who would just sit in the corner and take whatever was dished out. I was stronger and wiser because of what had happened to me.

As I sat there on that couch alone, I was reminded of the lesson that Viktor Frankl in his book, 'Man's Search for Meaning' had taught me after my car accident years earlier. I had a choice as to how I responded. I could react from fear. I could have been angry, cursed her, blamed her for all the wrongs in my life and given up on everything. But just as before I chose to respond from love.

My heart was leading me to help the children at Bulamu Children's Village where Geofrey and Ivan had grown up. I was not sure how I was going to do it. After all, my life had been reduced to a suitcase, I had little money. However, one thing I was sure of, the will of one single person is stronger than any atomic bomb, if they stay focused on the goal.

The writings that I had started at Ivan and Joe's apartment were now finished. The book 'Lead with your Heart' was released. It is the story of what led up to me leaving with just a suitcase, and how I became connected to Geofrey and Uganda. After its release, I had a bunch of copies shipped to me that I put in my purse. On my days off from the hospital, I took copies of my book to media outlets, radio stations, and newspapers all over Las Vegas. It was a way to get my story out and to begin to build my foundation. The love for those children kept me going when nothing else could. I was determined to help Joseph Lubega, the founder of Bulamu, continue the work with those children. Some of it panned out and interviews began to flood in.

I picked up extra shifts at the hospital, and after a few months, I had saved some money. I had written a bucket list while in Minnesota, a list of things I always wanted to do and places I wanted to see. Of course, going to Uganda to see Geofrey and to meet the people whose lives had been changed by Geofrey through AMKA Foundation Africa was number one on that list. It was time for me to break out of the cocoon to be the beautiful butterfly I was meant to be.

CHAPTER 6:

Martha Gets Her Groove Back.

When caterpillar researchers help
butterflies escape their cocoons, it results
in the butterfly having misshapen wings.
Self-education, and self-discovery is
important to your success.

-Martha Hoy

I packed up my suitcase one early morning in
March 2019. By then I had come into the fashion sense that I would become known for, it
was like my wardrobe change. As a nurse, it is
scrubs, a ponytail and comfortable shoes. But
as this character, Mother Martha, it was high
heels, tight jeans, designer blouses, and big ear-
rings, hair and makeup to perfection. I never
knew I had any fashion sense. But then again,
I lived most of my life being told who I was.

When I boarded a plane at McCarran International Airport in Las Vegas early that morning, little did I know I was embarking on the
journey of a lifetime. As I buckled my seatbelt
listening to the flight attendants give safety instructions, a smile came over my face when I
heard this was a non-stop flight to New York
City. New York, the perfect place to see the

landmarks of the United States. My ultimate destination was Uganda, but I had many things to mark off on my list during this trip.

On my lap was a T-shirt that said Las Vegas on the front. I had bought it for my friend, John "Happy" Bagenda in Uganda. John grew up in Bulamu Children's Village. He was one of the first children that Joseph Lubega took in as a child to the orphanage. We became instant friends; it was like we had known each other for years from the first moment we talked. John had been helping Geofrey at AMKA Foundation Africa since its beginning in 2017. We acted so much alike that people started to call us twins. His nickname was 'Happy' for obvious reasons. During our FaceTime chats we would tell each other jokes and spend most of our time laughing. I loved our time together; we were comfortable with each other. For the first time in my life, I could be myself with someone else, with no expectations, no strings, and no games. Just enjoying talking to each other, and I was looking forward to us spending time together in Uganda.

My relationships with men most of my life had not been picture perfect, my father was an alcoholic and my ex-husband abusive. But my friendship with John, even my connection with Geofrey, taught me how men and women should interact with each other. I learned that someone far away can be closer to you than someone who is sitting next to you.

Connections make us feel lifted, but attachments make us feel drained. I learned that both communication and connection was necessary for a healthy relationship.

First stop was New York City. I had a few places to mark off on my stop: The Metropolitan Museum of Art, the Statue of Liberty, the New York Harbor, Broadway, and Times Square. All the iconic things that make it the "the Big Apple." A city so legendary that songs and books have been written about it.

I hesitated to see the September 11th Memorial, because of all the emotions around it. Every American that lived through that day can tell you where they were, the moment they heard that two planes hit the Twin Towers, killing almost 3,000 people and injuring nearly 6,000 people. It was devastating. The news filled our homes with images of devastation. The thought that any human could hold that much evil within them still haunts me. It tore a nation apart, but Americans have a great spirit, it in the end it brought us together.

Many emotions came to me when seeing the sights of New York. The Statue of Liberty and the smell of New York Harbor made me think about the people that came to the United States in search of a dream. Times Square where people seemed to be rushing around eager to go somewhere. The food in New York City does not compare to any where else in the world. I had no problem finding pizza and Coca-Cola. It was just two days of sightseeing, but New York did not disappoint.

I boarded a plane at JFK with the end destination of Dubai. United Arab Emirates, the Middle East, quite a cultural change from where I had been living in Las Vegas. I had a friend living in Dubai named Sadat. I met Sadat while helping Geofrey with AMKA Foundation Africa. Sadat, around 30 years old, tall and slender from Uganda had been bullied out of Uganda, exiled into Dubai. I understood how he felt to exiled because I was forced from my home as well just a year earlier. Many Ugandans and people from East Africa leave for the Middle East in search of a better life. My friend Sadat, however, was forced out of his home and ended up in Dubai.

Sadat was exiled for speaking his mind. He could no longer deal with the opposition he saw around him. It is difficult for me to understand what it is like to live in a place where speaking your mind can get you jail time or even killed. That is the truth for people in Uganda and in many countries in the world. Many Ugandans have told me as children they are told "watch what you say the government can hear you, the walls have ears." A fear of the government instilled in them from childhood.

Sadat's father had been a wealthy businessman in Uganda until the current leadership came into power. It is what dictators do. They take out those they feel will keep them from retaining in power. He had enough of living life under fear. As a child his father was dropping him off for school when he was shot in the leg. The bullet was intended for his father but missed him and hit 11-year-old Sadat in the leg. The authorities came to arrest the rest of his family. His younger sister lost her life, her body was found in a dustbin not long after the arrest. In Uganda, a dustbin is the area where the trash is taken out. Her body disposed of like a bag of trash as if she were not human. Sadat's father was arrested by the government, and never seen again after his arrest. All the wealth his father had accumulated was taken and he was arrested. No one heard or saw his father again after his arrest. His mother and grandmother raised the children on what they had left they best they could.

Sadat now around 30 years old was tired of the state of his country; he began to speak his mind. Men broke into his home and there was a failed attempt to kill him. Just like me, he ran with little belongings. He went where he knew people and where he could make a fresh start. He started a charitable foundation in Uganda to help children while he was living in Dubai. That is how we became friends; we both love children and have a passion for helping in Uganda.

I will never forget landing in Dubai, as soon as I exited that plane, I felt the hot humid hit me in the face, then took my breath. After all,

I lived in Las Vegas where the air is dry. Having Multiple Sclerosis sometimes a change in climate will cause symptoms to flare up. I had jet lag from going across five time zones. My legs hurt and I had shortness of breath when I was walking through the jetway. Having had 15 surgeries, in addition, I have Multiple Sclerosis, I was grateful that shortness of breath was the only symptom that I was experiencing.

Once again, I found myself waiting at the airport to be picked up by someone I had only seen in pictures or over my phone. I stood at the pickup area of Dubai International Airport looking around for Sadat.

The culture change began in the airport, the Arabic writing on the signs, the modest clothing, and the music playing overhead. After all, I was used to Las Vegas, one of the most liberal places on Earth. I had done my research on Islamic law before I bought the plane ticket. Being a single woman traveling alone to a Middle Eastern country ruled by Islamic law, it was only common sense to know the laws and rules there before hand.

The sight of Sadat caught my eye as I scanned the crowd of people, he was the only person not dressed in traditional Islamic dress. I wanted to hug him right away. After all I am from the southeast United States and we hug people. I even say, "I am going to hug the bananas out of you when I see you" to anyone I have not seen in a while. That saying really does not make sense, but does any common saying from anywhere make sense?

Public displays of affection are not just frowned upon but a reason to be jailed under Islamic law, so I did not dare hug my friend. We exchanged smiles and pleasant greetings as he took my suitcase, to load into his car. Sadat drove me to my hotel, again something that frowned upon under Islamic law, two people of the opposite sex are not allowed to be alone together unless married or related. No one was going to believe we were related, for obvious reasons. I like Sadat but I was not about to marry him. I did not feel unsafe that he was driving me to my hotel with Dubai being a little more liberal than the rest of the Middle East due to tourist.

The sights of downtown Dubai were amazing to me. Not like the bright lights of Las Vegas but magnificent just the same. When we were in the car, I was looking out the windows more than talking to my friend. Which might have come off as rude in that culture, but it something that I had done since the car accident. Once you lose the ability to see the world around you. That is something you never take for granted again. I was amazed at the sites of Dubai.

While in the car Sadat began to point out the different landmarks as we drove past them. Burj Al Arab, the Dubai Mall, and the Dubai fountains. The people were dressed in traditional Islamic attire, the beautiful bright colors worn by women were dazzling to the eyes. Because I had been living in Las Vegas, I did a comparison in my mind as we drove; the fountains of the Bellagio are much more impressive, and the clothing you see on the streets of Vegas are anything but conservative. I respect other people's cultures and emotions, so I bought a hijab before I left on my trip; it was purple, my favorite color. I was ready to explore this beautiful city and spend time with my friend. Dubai was already impressive to me just from my ride from the airport to my hotel.

I think people go into other countries expecting they will behave or live the same as they do in their home countries. Impressive as Dubai is, no one should ever expect to act in the same manner in Dubai as they would in a place like Las Vegas. If you do then expect to be jailed in the Middle East. We should always respect the cultures, traditions, and emotions of others but especially when you are guest in their country, town, or home.

As Sadat pulled up to my hotel, we agreed that he would pick me up later after I got settled into my room. Flying across five time zones is difficult on the body. My body had been through 15 surgeries and has Multiple Sclerosis. Neither of those things stopped me much. I never claim to be a victim of either, because once you claim that you are a victim of something then it can control you. On a daily basis, I know what I need to do to adjust my lifestyle.

Sadat picked me up a few hours later. He was going to show me Dubai, his version of Dubai. He lives there, and he knows that city. I like to explore places with people that live there; I think you get a more authentic experience. Sadat was my friend; we had a lot of catching up to do. He decided to take me to an American restaurant. Not sure why since I live in the United States and get enough of that experience. But it was interesting to taste American food in the Middle East.

I quickly learned to lower my voice in public. I like to laugh and tell jokes. My laugh is quite loud and unique. Sadat had to tell me many times to please lower my voice. However, in his defense sometimes people must tell me that in the United States as well. We sat and talked about his work in Uganda with orphans. I shared with him what I planned to do in the future with Mother Martha Family Foundation. My overall goal was to take all the negative things that had happened to me and turn them into something good. By helping the children of Bulamu Children's Village where Ivan and Geofrey grew up in Kampala, Uganda,

The children in Bulamu are my "why." The thought of helping them kept me going when I did not think there was a shred of hope left. When it all felt too difficult to continue, the love I have for those children kept me going. They had become the meaning for it all.

After eating we decided to take a walk. I agreed because it was such a beautiful city from the car, I figured on foot it would be much more impressive. I put on my purple hijab to prepare to walk the city. Sadat informed me that in the tourist areas such as the spice market, the gold market and places downtown it was not necessary to adorn one. Nevertheless, I felt it was the right thing to do.

We walked and talked for a while on the sidewalk and found ourselves in this park. It was beautiful. People were out enjoying the cool evening. Like Las Vegas it is a desert climate but much more humid that Las Vegas. Coming out of the plane the humidity took my breath for a moment. However, the weather was perfect for an evening walk. The thing that stood out to me was people were walking cats on leashes like they would walk their dogs in the evening in the United States. I turned to Sadat and said, "Are they walking their cats?" Sadat grinned and said, "Yes they are walking their house cats" as if nothing were odd to him about it. I said "Well Darlin' where I come from our cats stay in the house, if they go outside, we just open the door and let them go outside." "We walk our dogs like that." To him that seemed a little odd. My final thought on it was "How do you get a cat to put on a leash?" "The cat I had for years,

Gizmo, was grumpy. He scratched and fought me just putting a collar around his neck." We just agreed that both things seemed odd to us and continued with our lovely evening stroll in the park.

After our walk Sadat stated that he was tired and ready to go home for the night. He decided he would hail a cab for me to take back to my hotel. He stepped out to the curb to hail a cab with no response for a while. It seemed odd to me. But I had been there for less then 24 hours maybe it was not odd for Dubai. It was completely different than what I was used to back in the states. After he tried for several minutes a cab stopped. The driver got out, stood next to his car, and lit a cigarette. Then he approached us. I do not understand Arabic, but I understood that whatever he was saying he had a problem with us. Pure anger on his face. Human emotions, especially anger, are recognizable across all cultures.

Next thing I knew Sadat looked at me and stated, "Let's go!" in a forceful tone. He turned and began to walk in the direction away from the man. I followed him after all I trusted him, and I was in an unfamiliar part of the world. I walked quickly to get caught up with him, I said, "What did he say?" Sadat turned to me and said, "Martha he is an ignorant man. He refused to give us a ride because I was a white woman with an African man." We walked to my hotel; Sadat then got a cab home.

As I returned to my hotel room, I got ready for bed. I really was not shocked by the man's reaction to us. Racism is everywhere and it is quite simply ignorance. Not sure why people think racism it is just a white and black issue or even just in their country. How can we stop such ignorance? Not sure that we can change the world on that one. Just like with everything else, change begins within us. If we want to end the separation between people reach out to another, especially to someone who you perceive as different than us.

The next morning, we decided to go to all the main tourist areas in Dubai. Those are on what is called the European side. The part you see on the commercials. I am not much into shopping, but I wanted to see the Dubai mall. Most people that know me well would say I am frugal. Not cheap, but frugal. I understand the difference between price and value. Something can be overpriced compared to its value. I like to think it is a skill set. I have always been frugal that came in handy when I was putting Geofrey through law school.

The worlds tallest building, Burj Khalifa, was next on my list. By the time I got to the top, I could mark off one more thing. I went as far up to the top of the worlds tallest building that they would allow me to go. I had a feeling of excitement increased as I went to up the building. The view from there is breathtakingly beautiful of the city below. I could now mark more things off my list. I had one more day with my friend which made me a bit sad. Nevertheless, my next stop was where my heart truly is always, Uganda.

Waking up in the Middle East to the sound of the people in the mosques singing is quite amazing. I have always believed that every faith is just a branch off the same tree. One God with many different paths to the creator. Each person has their own path. Every master taught the same lesson, love. Where there is love there is God and where there is God there is love. Although I am not of the Muslim faith, the signing brought a peacefulness to my heart.

On my day in Dubai with Sadat we spent it on what is called, the African/Indian side. A part of Dubai you do not see in commercials. It is called that for obvious reasons, people from Africa and India come there to settle. I was excited about visiting there because I was looking forward to trying the food. I love food, but the two things that always make my heart happy are Coca-Cola and pizza. I tried both at every placed I have ever been, Dubai was no different.

As we walked the streets of Dubai, I noticed a park with a lot of African men in it. They were sleeping on benches. Something I had not seen on the European side of Dubai. When I asked Sadat about it, he said many young African men end up there. They come to Dubai in search of a better life. However, they do not always find the opportunity they came for and they end up desperate living in this park. Many of them selling their passports for food. I am tender hearted, the sight of these men made me burst out in tears. The desperate looks on their faces seem to pierce right into my soul.

As the tears stream down my face. I knew the only thing I could do was give them a meal. A temporary solution, but it was something I could do to help. Sadat being bilingual helped me to speak to these young East African men many from Uganda.

It was my last evening in Dubai, I was trying to shake off the bad feelings I had from seeing those men in the park. Sadat then suggested we met some of his friends at a local restaurant. We spent the last evening together laughing, eating, and enjoying each other's company.

The next morning, we said goodbye at the airport. Goodbyes are always difficult, but I knew we would see each other again. We could not hug each other as I departed for my flight to Uganda, but we did take a picture with each other in the airport. I will always treasure that moment.

As I boarded the plane in Dubai for Uganda, I still felt a sadness in my heart leaving Sadat. I enjoyed my time in Dubai and I learned a lot about the culture and the people. I got closer to my friend. I knew I would be packing my suitcase to visit Dubai again. Then a wave of excitement came over me with the thought that in just 6 hours, I would be in Uganda with Geofrey. Geofrey and I continued to talk while I was in Minnesota and Las Vegas. We talked less than we ever did before because he was busier. He was running AMKA Foundation Africa and starting his life. Nevertheless, we were always staying in contact with one another.

With great anticipation I began to look out the window as we were beginning our ascension from Dubai International airport. Winston Churchill called Uganda the pearl of Africa. I was full of excitement to see Uganda and wrap my arms around Geofrey, my heart on two legs.

Six hours later, I looked out the window of the plane; Entebbe, Uganda came into sight. The beautiful landscape around Lake Victoria was stunning, the small huts with children playing outside. The adults tending to the animals. As they announced our landing in 20 minutes to Entebbe International Airport my anticipation grew. I had traveled 10,000 miles; I was feeling jet lagged but nothing could lesson my feelings of excitement. Twenty minutes later the door opened of the plane opened and as I stepped out to walk down the stairs. I remembered how humid the air was in Dubai and how it took my breath when I exited the plane. I prepared myself for the same feeling. After all it was East Africa; it is a tropical humid climate. Once again, I felt short of breath. My legs were weak just the same, but the shortness of breath did not last longer more a few seconds.

I exited the plane to Entebbe International Airport, in Uganda. My friend Francis would be waiting for me at the airport. Francis was Geofrey's best friend and I knew I could trust him. He had been running AMKA Foundation Africa with Geofrey since it is start in 2017. In two years, Francis had proven he was a good businessman and a trusted friend to Geofrey and I both. My relationship with Francis is much different then with Geofrey. Geofrey and I are more like Mother and son. But Francis and I, we tell jokes, laugh, and pick on each other like siblings. Geofrey does not have much of a sense of humor, he is quiet and soft-spoken. The strong, silent type of guy. But Francis and I share the same silly sense of humor. Nevertheless, when there is business to be done, we get serious and we get things done.

International airport might be a bit of a stretch to call Entebbe's airport. I guess it does get international flights coming in to get that title but at first sight of it, I stated, "Well this looks like my Pap Paw's chicken coop back in West Virginia." Of course, I had been living in Las Vegas with its glitz and glamour the past two years. I went through the line for international visitors and picked up my suitcase. I exchanged some of my United States Dollars for Ugandan shillings then went to the passenger pick up area.

Now we can not ignore the fact I am a white lady that went into an African country by myself. Some would say that was brave. I felt nothing but pure excitement about being in Uganda. After all these are the people that were there for me when I need someone when I was on the other side of the planet. If they were there for me when I was 7,000 miles away, then I felt safe in being in their immediate presents.

Seems that many twists and turns in my life have happened at airports. This one seemed like the most exciting of them all. I walked outside to the passenger pick up and I stood there with my suitcase scanning the crowd for Geofrey's face. As I looked around my heart was racing with anticipation. A few minutes later Geofrey stepped out of the crowd. My heart sunk, I dropped everything, and I ran to him. I threw my arms around him. He threw his arms around me. Tears came down my face.

Not tears of sorrow but tears of joy. It was like time stood still. Noise of the people rushing around us continued but for us it seemed as though time stood still. I could not let go. I did not want to let go.

After a few minutes Francis, Geofrey's best friend, came forward and tapped us on the shoulder. He said, "Okay you two. Our ride is here. We have to get Martha to her hotel in Entebbe." Still not wanting to let go of Geofrey I picked up my suitcase and held his hand. Geofrey looked at me and spoke for the first time, "I can not believe you are here!" I stated, "I certainly cannot believe I am here, but I am grateful." Francis took my suitcase to load in his car. I was still holding onto Geofrey's hand as we walked to the car.

The drive from the airport to my hotel, Frontier Hotel in Entebbe was better than what I expected. Just like in Dubai, I found myself looking out the windows instead of talking to those around me. I was taking in the scenery of Uganda. It is like God painted this picture just for us. Untouched by humans in many places. It was more amazing than I had ever imagined it would be. Beautiful trees, greenery, and the sky a beautiful clear blue.

The areas were people lived were completely opposite compared to Las Vegas. Dirt roads, women carrying baskets on their heads, and many people driving motorcycles. Not just one person or two people on a motorcycle but up to 5 people on some motorcycles. Many of them children with no helmets. As a nurse, I was horrified. I wanted Francis to stop the car so I could get out and say, "Be safe! Put helmets on, put helmets on those children!" I guess that is why I got the nick name Momma Martha, always mothering everyone. Francis said, "Those are called Boda Bodas here." I said "Lawd, they look unsafe to me darlin'. As a nurse, I am ready to get out and enforce safety rules." Everyone in the car began to laugh at me trying to be a mother to the entire town of Entebbe.

Francis had been Geofrey's best friend for a few years. My friendship with Francis was a silly one. We like to tell jokes and laugh, not like my relationship with John or Geofrey. Francis and I have a silly picking on each other sibling type of relationship. The jokes can get a little off the collar. In the car on the way to my hotel, I looked at Francis and stated, "behave yourself." Everyone in the car laughed when I said it, I think they must know why I was saying that to Francis. I am sure his off the collar jokes have been around for a while.

We pulled into the driveway at Frontiers Hotel, at 8 Mugwanya Road, less than a half of a mile to the State House of Uganda, and a view of Lake Victoria. At that moment, I had no idea this place would end up feeling like my home away from home. The people that work there would become my friends. It is a small hotel with walls around the boarder of the property made of blocks with barbed wire on the top. At the beginning of the driveway is a guard house before you get to the entrance of the hotel. The landscape typical of East Africa, tropical trees, and green grass. I knew when I stepped out of the car and saw the pizza place on the grounds of the hotel that this was my place. My love of Coca-Cola and pizza is one love affair that has never been broken. After checking into the hotel, we all agreed I should rest. The following day was already packed with activities. Jet lag was starting to affect me: headache, fatigue, and upset stomach. I gave Geofrey a hug goodbye. For Francis, it was one of our silly jokes, and a "see you tomorrow."

I sat my suitcase on the bed and went to the sliding glass doors that lead to the balcony. As I moved the curtain to the side, the view of Lake Victoria revealed itself. I opened the door to walk out on the balcony. The view was too spectacular not to get a better look.

I could hear the birds chirping, the sounds from the farm animals close by, and the sight and sounds of the monkeys playing in the trees. The sun was setting over the lake. At that moment, I forgot about being jetlagged, my heart was at peace. The best way to describe it is that it was a feeling of, "I am home."

I spoke out loud to myself, "This is why Winston Churchill called Uganda the pearl of Africa." The sights and sounds of the shores of Lake Victoria became imprinted on my heart and soul.

The room was basic, the floor was tiled, and the bed linens had elephants and giraffes on them. On the side was a desk with an outdated computer on it. There was a television mounted on the wall. Big closets to the side. There was an air conditioner, one of those small units, which worked quite well. Having MS, staying cool is important. Heat intolerance is a common symptom of Multiple Sclerosis. The bathroom had an open shower, and a small sink. I liked that there was a sky light so that the African sun can shine in on you as you shower. I prepared for bed that night with a peaceful heart and a bit of excitement for what was to come the next day. Geofrey had talked to me from Bulamu Children's Village for many years, and I was about to see the place he had so vividly described. I was going to meet the people whose lives I had indirectly changed through Geofrey at AMKA Foundation Africa. I drifted into a peaceful sleep to the sounds of Lake Victoria.

In the morning I was woken up by a phone call from Francis that he could not pick me up that morning to take me to AMKA Foundation. I got dressed and went down to the restaurant for breakfast. A spread of fresh fruits, and breads was sitting out on a table to the side of the sitting area. As I sat down a very well-dressed young lady came out of the kitchen and asked me if I wanted an omelet for breakfast. Since I had seen chickens on the property the evening before my answer was an immediate, "Yes please." In the United States we have labels on dozens of eggs that say, "free range." In Uganda all the chickens are free range chickens. I come to learn later, that chickens come and go as they please. Even making an appearance in the bank when I was in line to make a withdraw.

When the young lady bought the omelet to the table, I asked her if she knew of any drivers that could drive me to Kampala this morning, on short notice. The distance from Entebbe to Kampala they said was about 54 km. I had no idea how far that was; we do not use the metric system in the United States. Regina the young lady I meet working the front desk came to tell me that Kampala was a 50-minute drive away and that they would call Sam, a driver that she knew well. She stated, "Sam lives not far from here in Entebbe and he might be able to drive you on short notice."

Just 30 minutes later very tall, muscular young man walked into the restaurant introducing himself as Sam that he was there to drive me to Kampala. The accents of people in Uganda make everything they say sound proper. Until 1962, Uganda was under the rule of the British. They speak the Queen's English. I speak more like Paula Dean, the TV cook from the southeast United States. Living in Las Vegas was starting to take the twang out of my voice. There was enough left for people to say, "oh that is kind of cute." Not sure I agree with that, but it does not sound as proper as the Queen's English. As I shook Sam's hand, he asked for the directions to AMKA.

I said "Darlin' I have no idea. I am from Las Vegas. I don't even know where in the world I am right now." "But let me call Francis and he will tell you how to get there." Sam spoke to Francis on the phone, and we agreed on a price for him to be my driver for the day. After I finished my omelet, we set off for AMKA Foundation Africa.

Geofrey had started AMKA Foundation Africa to "pay it forward." When I told him that I would put him through law school the only thing I asked was that he do something kind for someone else. In Uganda if an orphan did get to go to an orphanage then once his graduated out of the orphanage, they had no skills and no way to support themselves. AMKA gives young people job skills.

At AMKA they teach hair dressing, cosmetology, computing, and fashion design courses. Geofrey came up with the idea for the fashion design course from the stories I used to tell him about my neighbor, Camilla. She taught me how to sew as a teenager. My parents were factory workers in West Virginia so growing up we did not have the money for me to dress like the popular girls at school. My next-door neighbor Camilla, a retired seamstress taught me to make my own clothes and to modify clothing I found in secondhand stores. It was beneficial to Camilla and me. She was alone all day in the house, her children had moved to Texas, she enjoyed passing on her skills, and I enjoyed my time with her. What Camilla taught me I still use today. The influence my neighbor had on me from years ago is still going forward today, not only through me but through the ladies at AMKA Foundation.

In the parking lot of Frontier Hotel, Sam opened the back door of a late model Toyota. When I got in the car first thing, I noticed was the piece cloth that looked like fur covering the dashboard. He got in the driver's seat which to me was the wrong side. The steering wheel is on the right and people drive on the left side of the road. The British way of driving. When I inquired about the fur on his dashboard Sam stated it was there to cut down on the dust. I said, "Makes sense because of the dirt roads." Then I began to look out of the windows as we pulled past the guard house coming out of the hotel driveway.

Sam reached up and pushed a button on the radio. The familiar sound of Dolly Parton's song 'Coat of many Colors' got my attention. I said, "Do you like Dolly Pardon?" Sam said, "Ms Parton is one the most popular singers in Uganda." I leaned forward toward the front seat with a look of shock on my face. "Really?" I said with surprise in my voice. Sam said, "The song, 'When I think about love' is the most played love song in Uganda. It is played at weddings, dances, and anywhere there are lovers."

I said, "That is amazing." "I grew up on Dolly Pardon's music." "Hmm… it really is a small world." "Well then, let's enjoy some Dolly on the way to AMKA." We played our favorite Dolly Pardon music for the hour trip to AMKA as I looked out the window enjoying the scenery. Sam and I periodically along the way. The usual getting to know you type stuff, where did you grow up, and how is your family. After just an hour of talking to this man I had just met, we had a lot in common.

He had lived in Dubai, which I had just come from that area. We discussed what we had both experienced there. We like the same movies, music and traveling. He was happy in a relationship with a young lady named Brenda. That was where our commonalities ended. I told him briefly about my love life and that subject ended with the statement "I have no desire to date." He said "Okay" with a look on his face like 'we will not go there with that subject of conversation.'

We pulled into a neighborhood in Kampala about an hour later. It was the poorest neighborhood I had ever seen. Dirt roads, dwellings made of cardboard with tin roofs. There were slabs of meat just hanging outside with flies swarming them. Children playing in around the dwellings with holes in their clothing. It was a sight I was not prepared for. At that moment I remembered to check to see if I had taken my daily dose of the malaria prevention medication that my doctor back in Las Vegas had prescribed for me. Female mosquitoes are the deadliest animals on the planet and malaria is a major problem in Uganda. I will never forget the sight of that neighborhood. Geofrey said he started AMKA Foundation there because it was where the need was the greatest. I understood why he picked this neighborhood when I saw it with my own eyes.

Sam pulled in front of an entrance with a big closed wooden door. Block fences and security doors are the normal in Uganda, so the large security door was not alarming to me. A young man came to the door and swung it open. The sign to AMKA was large outside an orange building. I was feeling a little anxious to meet everyone. Feeling of butterflies in my stomach had begun as I got out of Sam's car. A group of young ladies greeted me after I got out of the car carrying a big bouquet of orange flowers. Orange was the color that Geofrey had chosen for AMKA uniforms. A mentor of mine, who had passed on a few years earlier, loved orange. Seeing those young ladies looking so beautiful in their uniforms made me smile thinking of my mentor. The wisdom she passed down to me was worth more than any gold in the world. The students wearing her color was sort of in remembrance of her to me.

I took the flowers from students as they said, "Welcome." I did not know if it were proper to hug them or even if they could speak English. I thought education might be an issue there, but the assumption was based on what I had seen on the way there. I do like to 'hug the bananas out of people' after all. Geofrey comes out of the front door of AMKA and hugs me. He states, "Everyone speaks English Momma Martha." He must have seen the puzzled look on my face and figured out what I was thinking. A little boy that looked about 4 years old came running to me. Then stopped and looked up as if he were surprised. Geofrey said, "I think this is the first time he has ever seen a white person." It honestly never entered my mind that someone there may have never seen a white person before. I had always lived in the United States;

we are a country of people of many races and cultures.

He spoke to Geofrey in a language I did not understand. He asked Geofrey if I was an angel or a devil. It did not bother me, after all from the mouths of babes. I put down the flowers and smiled at him. Reached out my arms as if to hug him. A gesture anyone can understand no matter race, culture, or language. We all understand a smile and a hug, showing someone a bit of kindness. The next thing I knew that young man was in my arms and I was carrying him around. I think he figured out I was not a devil.

That is when I learned the word Mzungu. It is not a term of racism. Mzungu literally translates to mean "foreigner." It is just a matter-of-fact description to say this person has light skin or the person is not of African heritage.

Geofrey then took me to the area where the fashion design course was being taught. He introduced me to Ruth, the teacher of that course. I had recognized her from the pictures that Geofrey had sent me. Everyone at AMKA looked young but Uganda is a country in which 70% of the population is under the age of 35. Ruth showed me how she taught the students to sew before they even used any material. The fabric was expensive, so she them taught to sew with thick paper first, before cutting into the fabric. They had 7 sewing machines and 30 students, but they were making do with what they had.

The ladies at AMKA in the hairdressing course wanted to style my hair. I understood the curiosity, my hair being a different texture. I welcomed it because my hair was frizzy from the humidity. Because the buildings had European electrical plugs, I did not get to use any a straightening iron or curling iron I brought with me from the United States. The hair styles there are amazing to me, the different braids, and the sparkly hair barrettes in their hair. The women in their culture seemed to support each other more than what I am used to in the United States. Women in the United States can be very catty and mean to each other. In the south east, if someone says 'bless your heart" honey they are not really trying to bless you. It is a passive-aggressive way to insult you.

Francis came out to the class and ushered me down a small hallway into a small office. It had a desk and a living room furniture set up. I sat down in a big fluffy couch that I seem to sink into. Francis and Geofrey wanted to share with me what AMKA had been doing since its start in December 2017. It was amazing to me how many people's lives were affected positively. I proudly looked out at Francis, and Geofrey has they talked about the students of AMKA past and present. They talked about their plans to add more classes such as auto repair and welding. That they needed more computers for the computer class. They asked the students to pay it forward after they graduated from their classes. By then they had graduated three classes since each course is 6 months long. Asking the students to pay it forward lead to one student coming back to teach classes. After graduating several students, started their own businesses in which they came back to hire other students.

After coming out of the office Geofrey had me speak to all the students. It put me on the spot because I was not prepared to speak to everyone. I gave a short speech on how I was proud of everyone there for acting on improving their lives. That I would help them in any way I could because their success is important to me. At that moment I realized I was seeing how one kind act that I did a few years earlier had grown to affect many more people in a positive way. I was in awe at that moment. I was so proud of Geofrey, he had 'paid it forward' more than I could have ever imagined he would.

Sam and I drove back to my hotel in Entebbe late that evening. As I looked out the windows of Sam's car at the setting sun the beautiful Ugandan sunset, I was saying a little prayer to myself that I hope that AMKA could continue to positively affect people in Kampala for a long time to come.

As I prepared for bed that evening, I was enjoying watching it rain from the balcony of my hotel. As I lay in the bed of my hotel room, I started to feel pain in my feet and knees. The pain in my feet is chronic, I have had little relief from it since the accident. The rains in Africa are very soothing, the sound is almost magical to my ears. Living in the desert of Las Vegas the last few years, I had seen little rain. It felt like a blessing to listen to the rain as I drifted off to sleep.

The next morning, I woke up to my phone ringing, and it was Daniel on the other end. Daniel is a film producer and photographer. I hired him to take some pictures for the day. I was going to Bulamu Children's Village to see where Geofrey had been talking to me from. We began talking daily in 2014 when he was an orphan at Bulamu. Finally, I was getting to see, feel and experience the place Geofrey had described to me.

Waking up on the shores of Lake Victoria is an experience difficult to describe the beauty of the pearl of Africa. It brought peace to my heart from the first moment I laid eyes on this area of the world. The smells and sounds there I can only describe as magical. It is like experiencing what the creator truly had in mind when the Earth was formed. The area is largely untouched by humans. I got ready for my day thinking of how grateful I was that Sam had agreed to drive me again. All the time we were spending together, it was the beginning of a wonderful friendship.

I got dressed to go to breakfast at the hotel restaurant. As I began to eat from the table of fresh fruits, the young lady came out of the kitchen and placed an omelet on the table in front of me. They were starting to know me after just a few days. Only 11% of the population in Uganda has access to electricity so most the food is fresh, due to few people having refrigerator or freezers. In the United States we use a lot of processed foods we put in the freezer that we can quickly put in a microwave when we are hungry. None of that here, the food was fresh not frozen.

After breakfast I went to the reception area where Sam had picked me up the morning before. While sitting there waiting for Sam, I gotten to know Regina the young lady that works the front desk. I love people and I love connecting with people. I do not always like them because of how people can be mean and cruel to each other.

As Sam and I were getting in his car he told me that he was driving me through Kampala again today. Kampala is the capital city of Uganda, driving through it for the first time the day before was an eye-opening experience. There are no traffic lights, no traffic lanes, no street signs, and hundreds of boda bodas going in every direction. It reminded me of the car scenes in the action movies that Matt Damon starred portraying the character, Jason Borne. Traffic going in all and any direction, the motorcycles carrying up to 4 or 5 people on them. Sometimes the Boda Bodas are weighed down carrying supplies. Cars and vans going in different directions. Totally chaotic yet some how people get to where they are going. Because of the economy, people hustle to make ends meet. The entrepreneurial sprit is there is a must, because they have to somehow feed their families. People coming up to the car window to sell you things is common.

As we were entering the traffic in downtown Kampala, a man approached the car window with an arm full of items. I bought a steering wheel cover from the man. Sam said, "Is that for your car back in Las Vegas." I said, "No it's for Geofrey." Sam replied "Geofrey does not have a car." "I know Sam." I said while handing the money to the man. "I am buying it for him as a reminder that he can reach his goal of owning a car." The man selling me the steering wheel cover looked at me and stated "You are buying this for someone that does not have a car? You must be drunk!" Sam and I burst out with loud laughter as we sit in the car. That steering wheel cover was placed on the wall of the office at AMKA Foundation Africa as a reminder to keep your eyes on the goal. You may have to change your approach, but the end goal always stays the same.

As we were at the edge of Kampala, Sam turned the car down this dusty country road. Big ruts in the road. Potholes big enough to lose your car in. It reminded me of my home in West Virginia. We used to make the joke that the state flower of West Virginia was a pothole in the road. The beauty on the roadside was beautiful. Green grass, beautiful forest as far as the eyes could see but quite a bumpy ride. I had been in Uganda a few days, but I had already noticed similarities to my home in West Virginia. The beautiful landscapes, the poorly maintained roads, and the downturn economy. The people much like back home, are so friendly and loving. I was just unfortunate that my life back in West Virginia, I was surrounded by mostly people of poor character and judgment. Most of the people in West Virginia are kind and welcoming. People of poor judgment and character can be found anywhere on the planet.

I told someone I was originally from West Virginia when we had made a stop along the way. This person started singing the song 'Country Roads' by John Denver. "Country roads take me home to the place I belong." and "Almost heaven West Virginia" were the only parts they knew. The face that they knew that song at all was shocking. Through his music John Denver had touched the hearts of many people and I just hope I can touch the hearts of many like he did in his lifetime.

The drive to Bulumu seemed to take several hours. I did not mind because I was taking in the beautiful scenery. Staring out the window and enjoying every second of God's beautiful artwork. Sam was playing music on the radio that we both enjoyed and every now and again we would enjoy having a laugh together. I learned by then Dolly Pardon music was always on standby in his car.

After what seemed like an hour we drove into area where there were many small houses in what seemed like the middle of nowhere. We pulled into a driveway where a big wooden door opened as we pulled into the driveway, similar to the door at AMKA foundation. As the gates opened, I could see children to our left playing soccer field. In the United States we call it soccer but in other countries it is called football. What we call football in the United States is much different than soccer. To our right of that driveway was a big building with a red tin roof. Considerably basic walls with no insulation. Joseph Lubega, the man that began Bulamu later told me that is where the children attend church services. Sam parked the car next to that building and we got out.

I was very eager to see where Geofrey had talked to me from all those years. As I got out of Sam's car a flood of memories entered my mind of the stories, he had told me about his life here. Then I thought about how much different Geofrey and I were right then in the moment compared to when he was talking to me from here. Then he was an orphan here and I was an abused woman in West Virginia. I was of proud of the progress we had made, how much we had learned and grew as people.

Children were playing around us but not paying us much mind. A man approached us that I recognized as Joseph Lubega, the man everyone loving calls "Uncle Joseph" approached us. He is the founder of Bulamu Children's

Village. He is a very respected man in his community, rightfully so because what he has done has positively affected thousands of people including me. As we stood there shaking hands, there were almost 900 children residing at Bulamu. He had already raised a generation of children that included Ivan and Geofrey. Uncle Joseph was taller than I expected. When he shook my hand, I felt I was in the presence of a strong but kind person. Not many people master of the art of being soft and strong. To me I was shaking the hand of an angel on Earth. Because of the character and values, he had instilled in Ivan and Geofrey I was still alive. I loved him as family at first sight. That is when he became my Uncle Joseph as well.

"Welcome sister Martha" Joseph said with a smile. I awkwardly reached out my arms to give him a big hug. After all his actions did help to save my life in the big picture. After the awkward hug I introduced Uncle Joseph to Sam. We began to walk around Bulamu as we talked. I was not prepared for what I saw next. I knew from Geofrey's stories that people were trying their best to help with what resources they have. What I imagined it to be from my American perspective was much better than what I saw that day. Geofrey had downplayed what he saw. He was telling me from a perspective of a young man that had lost his parents and was probably just grateful that he and Ivan was not homeless on the streets anymore.

The school rooms were just bare floors, no desks, no books, no paper, no pencils, and just a chalk board on the walls. Unlike in the US where tax dollars pay for public school parents must pay to educate their children. We were then directed outside to walk toward the children's sleeping area. As I turned my head, I felt a tug on my pant leg. I look down to see a little girl. She looked about 4 to 5 years old. She had no hair and was wearing an orange dress. I knew she was malnourished based on her appearance, as I nurse, I had seen it enough to know. "Hello young lady" I stated. She did not speak back. I did not pay attention to it at first. Maybe she just did not know English. She reached up to me and I reached out my hand, we began to walk hand and hand together. Uncle Joseph turned to me, "I see you have met Catherine." "Indeed, I think I just made a new friend," I stated with a smile on my face. Katherine and I followed beside Uncle Joseph hand and hand as he continued his tour.

As we walked to the sleeping area, I saw mattresses piled up outside the small houses we had seen from the entrance of Bulamu. Sam turned to ask why the mattresses had been placed there. Uncle Joseph plainly stated that during rainy season the water gets inside the houses. The mattress become wet and the children must place them outside in the sun to dry. I looked up at Uncle Joseph's face and said, "This is where Geofrey was talking to me

from?" "Not this particular house but yes one near here this one," stated Joseph. Tears began to flow down my face.

This was worse than what I had imagined it would be. After seeing the sights here and the day before the conditions around AMKA Foundation Africa, I started to wonder how these things can happen. I knew the answer probably lie in poor leadership and rooted in money. The greed of the human ego will put lining their pockets above human lives. Money is the symbol of control. It is what gets things moving in the world.

Putting money first and the lives of people second is something I never understood. Seems to me that money comes from people, through buying goods and services keeping economies going. One of my favorite authors, Zig Ziglar used to say, "You can have everything you want in life by helping others get what they want." He meant by solving people's problems through goods and services you will have abundance.

Jeff Bezos created Amazon on those principles. He put solving people problems first and taking smaller profits when he started his company. I know I love being able to order what I need from the comfort of my couch. It arrives as soon as the next day at my front door. Putting people first paid off for Mr. Bezos, his current worth is 182 billion USD. I think people are not willing to take less in the beginning to have more later. They want reward right now. It takes maturity and intelligence to sacrifice in the present to have a bigger reward later.

Anything can be used for construction or destruction depending on the person's character that is directing it. Money just like anything else it can be used for good such as: to build a business, help a friend, or take your date out to a nice dinner. It can used for destructive purposes. No need to list those, based on what I had seen in Uganda the leadership was doing nothing constructive.

With a quiver in my voice, I stated, "So tell me how the children get dressed in the mornings, where are their clothes, and who helps the little ones?" I said as a bit of a joke, "I know one man does not help 900 children get ready for school in the mornings. Just getting one up and going is quite a chore." Everyone laughed. "There are house mothers in each house, they help the children in that house prepare for the day. We pay teachers to come into the classrooms to teach. For each child we try to get them sponsors to help purchase the necessary books, uniforms and school supplies."

However, I knew from walking into the classrooms there that contained just a chalkboard on the wall, obtaining school supplies was a problem. We then walked to the garden area where the children learn to grow food it was located behind the living area. Once again, I found myself looking out at the landscape of Uganda with wonder. Catherine was still holding my hand as we walked. Uncle Joseph then said that feeding the children was the most challenging part of it all. That is when he showed us the area where the children eat, that is when Catherine finally let go of my hand in order to eat her lunch.

The area where the children eat is basically a spot on the ground. They get their food on plates and then find a spot to sit on the ground. All the stories that Geofrey told me about growing up here came flooding back. He talked frequently of going to bed on an empty stomach. Sleeping in a bed with 5 other children. Nevertheless, I knew Uncle Joseph and the rest of the adults here were trying their best to help all these children. It is not an easy feat that he took on. Uganda being a country of 40 million people with an average of 2.5 million orphans. They were doing the best they could for those children.

After eating the children attended church. Sam and I attended with them that day. Most of the church services were in Luganda, one of the local languages. Sam was kind enough to interrupt for me. Catherine found me in the pews, sat in my lap, and then fell asleep. After services I introduced myself to some of the house mothers. As I looked around, I saw Geofrey's smile in the crowd of people leaving the building. I walked up to him and said "Hey Geofrey." He said, "I did not know you were coming here today." Sam, Geofrey and I along with Catherine by my side went out to sit in the African sun together. We sat outside for a couple of hours talking and laughing. I got overheated from sitting in the sun. Multiple Sclerosis symptoms appear when we get overheated. My head began to hurt so I then asked Sam to drive me back to Entebbe to Frontiers hotel. I needed to rest, in the air conditioning after such a long emotional day.

I had many mixed emotions from that visit. I left a sadness in my heart to see how the children were living. But it was also heartwarming to see how people were trying their best to help them. The heart of the people there and love they have for those children is amazing. I experienced a mixture of feelings: sadness, respect, shock, and gratitude.

As Sam and I were pulling out of the driveway to begin our journey back to Entebbe down that country road that reminded me of my home in West Virginia, I began to cry. It all hit me at once, a big wave of emotions. Like a grand healing had begun. I thought back to when Geofrey and I were talking to each other during the time he lived at Bulamu. During the time Geofrey was living there in Bulamu, and I was living in West Virginia. At that same time, we were both living our own versions of a hellish life. Through our friendship and connection, we had helped each other to heal.

I was a white woman from the United States, a nurse from thousands of miles away. I was in an abusive relationship, and I was healing from my injuries from a car accident. Learning to live with Multiple Sclerosis. He was an orphan who had lost his parents. He and Ivan were homeless children living on the streets until Uncle Joseph picked them up and brought them here. Although we were completely different from the outside looking in. We found common ground between us and made a connection, a friendship, and a new family that lead to us both to healing. My passion to help Uncle Joseph in his mission grew that day. I was more determined than ever to help him through Mother Martha Family Foundation in Las Vegas.

After returning to my hotel, I asked Sam to let me rest for a few days. The trip to AMKA and the visit to Bulamu had exhausted me. But not the usual tired. When you have Multiple Sclerosis, it is a different type of tired. At times I can get all the rest I possibly can and still feel like I just ran a marathon. I never think about having MS until it causes pain. My fingers feet and legs periodically become numb. My feet hurt continuously. Never a break from the pain in my feet. After I was diagnosed, I gave myself 10 minutes to have a pity party. I had one, I cried, I screamed and then I said, "If you consider yourself a victim of something then it can control you." Now the pity party is over. When you have any chronic illness, you learn to adapt to life with it, but I do not consider myself disabled. I have the same ability as most people, I have learned to adapt my life to accommodate the symptoms.

Everything can be taken from us but one thing, how we chose to respond. Everything was taken from me. My life was reduced to a suitcase. My health, and the people around me rejecting me or abusing me. But I chose to respond with love. Now I had begun to build a new family. My health issues would never go away but they rarely stop me from doing what I wanted. I had begun to discover who I was as a person, and what my passion was in life.

I had met quite a cast of characters after leaving with that suitcase in 2018. One of them was Prince Fredrick Walugembe. His grandfather was the first President of Uganda named Edward Mutesa II. He helped Uganda gain its independence from the British. They celebrate their independence on October 9th every year much like the United States celebrates its independence from the British on July 4th every year. I found Mutesa's story to be quite fascinating. In many ways it mirrors my story. He was exiled from his home as the King of the Buganda Kingdom, forced to flee his home to save his life. He jumped the palace wall and went into exile in England.

I was forced from my home, running for my life, and my Ugandan family let me stay with them. The rest the story does not parallel. Him being an African King and me being a nurse from West Virginia. Nevertheless, after Prince Fredrick told his grandfather's story, I could relate to how his grandfather felt. The emotions he must have felt that I could relate to.

Prince Fredrick had reached out before along with some of his other family members about writing a book about his grandfather. I felt a connection to his story, so I was considering it. Fredrick invited me to visit him at Mengo palace in Kampala. Mengo is the palace that Mutesa built and the place he was exiled from by Idi Amin. No one can say the name Uganda without thinking of Idi Amin. He was the President of Uganda after Mutesa. Amin was known as cruel dictator yet has received a lot of attention. Seems the bad guy in the story has gotten a lot of glory especially internationally. However, Mutesa is still admired and celebrated in East African. He was a man of the people and for the people.

I was excited to get to see where this man lived, learn more about him and about the culture of the Buganda Kingdom. After all the entire country is named after the kingdom, the word Uganda is just the word Buganda with the B removed.

After a few days rest Sam was coming to pick me up to take me to the palace. As I stood there looking at the clothing hanging in the closet of my hotel room that I brought from Las Vegas, I thought, "What does a Las Vegas girl wear to a palace to meet an African Prince?" At that moment I realize how weird and wonderful my life had truly become, I was going to meet a Prince. I decided to dress just as I would in Las Vegas. I would show up as me, the person I had become after all the tragedy. High heels, blue jeans and a designer blouse, my uniform as "Mother Martha."

Sam picked me up in the front reception area as usual and to the chaotic traffic of Kampala we went once again. We approached an entrance unlike the ones that I had seen in other places in Uganda. When I asked about it, he said that it was the entrance to the palace for the reigning king of the Buganda Kingdom. The King is not allowed to go in circles, he is only allowed to go straight. This straight entrance was only for him. It seemed odd to me yet fascinating at the same time. I said to Sam "Darlin' I live in Las Vegas the only king we know is Elvis. The king of rock in roll." We both laughed out loud as we drove the circle around the king's entrance.

We parked in a parking lot of what looked like an office building. The building looked like it had been built in the 1960s. Many places in Uganda look as though it is stuck in a time warp. Because the last progressive leadership it had was in the 1960s, at least that is the way it seemed to me.

Fredrick was on speaker phone on the way there, giving us specific directions for when we arrived. First, to go to the reception area on the third floor and ask for him. He said, "Tell them that I am expecting you at 11:00 am to tour Mengo palace." I had asked him previously if I could take pictures at the sight. He stated, "Do you know who my grandfather was? You can take pictures anywhere when you are with me." I responded to Prince Fredrick like this, "My parents were factory workers from West Virginia, what does who your grandfather was have to do with me taking pictures at the palace?" In the US there are places that even the President is not allowed to take pictures due to national security." I had visited the United States Capital enough to know there were specific rules everyone had to follow for the greater good of the people. That is when Sam proceeded to tell Prince Fredrick, "Martha is not easily impressed." After spending all those days together, Sam was beginning to understand me.

We went to the third floor and asked for Prince Fredrick as he instructed. The receptionist asked us to take a seat in the reception area of the offices of the radio station and television station of the Buganda Kingdom. I barely recognize celebrities in the US, so I knew I would not recognize the celebrities of Uganda. The king himself could have come walking by, I would have not known who he was. But when Prince Fredrick entered the room, I knew who he was immediately. He looks just like his grandfather, if a movie is ever made about Edward Mutesa, his grandson is his twin. Killer smile, slim build, and dressed in a black suit and tie. He looked very handsome, just as you would imagine an African Prince.

He approached me and said, "Hello Martha, Welcome to the Buganda Kingdom," in his very proper British accent. I said "Nice to meet you Frederick. This is my friend Sam." Fredrick and Sam shook hands with Fredrick they began the get to know you type conversation, 'nice to meet you, where are you from' type stuff. Prince Fredrick then said "Lets walk this way, we will begin our tour with the radio station and the television station then go to the palace.

We walked to the first floor of the building to the radio station. He showed us where the most popular radio shows are recorded. While inside an empty studio we saw a record player, I was the only one that remembered when people had them. A pleasant memory of my grandmother came to me she had one in her living room when I was grown up, she played the Kenny Rogers song 'the gambler' some much we all grew tired of it. I met so many people during the tour of the radio station CBS FM, that I could not remember their names. But everyone was friendly and accommodating.

Prince Fredrick then leads us into a building next door, to BBS the kingdom's television station. He introduced me to the station manager. That gentleman took us into a studio where the most popular comedy show was being filmed. Luganda and English are spoken there, and the actors were speaking in Luganda. I could not understand anything they were saying but I was grateful for the experience.

We then exited the building to an outside veranda. It was large and on the left was a big tent set up with a big group of people underneath it. Sam had said he needed to use the bathroom, so we stopped for a moment leaving me alone with Prince Fredrick. There was a moment of silence then he said, "I cannot believe you are here all the way from Las Vegas." I said, "Well doll, you know my story and what Ivan and Geofrey did for me." Prince Fredrick nodded his head and smiled. Then he did something I never expected, he leaned forward to kiss me.

I did not fight it, a handsome Prince with a killer smile comes forward to kiss you, you kiss him back. Besides, I had not dated since I left my previous relationship. The thought really did not cross my mind. But it was on my mind as Prince Fredrick pressed his lips against mine. He then put his arm around my waist and pulled my body close to his. Just then in that moment Sam came out to find us. We awkwardly pulled away from each other, trying to pretend nothing had happened.

Fredrick grabbed my hand, "Now come over here and let's take our picture in front of the statute of King Mutebi, my Uncle." Sam was just looking over at me as if he were holding back teasing me about the kiss he had accidentally witnessed as he took a picture of us. After taking our picture in front of the statue of the King, I noticed on our left were tents with a large amount of people sitting in chairs.

It looked like a party. People were happy and dressed in beautiful clothing, it was all very colorful and festive. Fredrick then turned his head toward Sam and I, "To our left is where people from the kingdom come every Wednesday to bring a gift to the King." "To the front of us is the mile of road that on each side is a piece of land where each clan within the kingdom has placed things that represent their clan. It is called the Royal Mile." Fredrick turned to Sam then stated, "Can you please go get the car, bring it around so that we can drive down the royal mile to Mengo palace."

This was when I really began to have a real interest in our tour. Now the kiss from the handsome Prince was good, but I was eager to see where Edward Mutesa had to flee from to save his life. I had lived through the same not long ago, so I felt a connection to his story. A person can understand how something feels when they have experienced it for themselves.

Having to run out of primal fear, not knowing where you can go and not knowing who you can trust with your life. At times not knowing where your next meal will come from or where you will lay your head down at night. It is an experience I do not wish on anyone. Not even those that caused it for me.

Sam pulled around the car, Prince Fredrick and I got in the backseat. We were leaving the administration building of the kingdom when then began driving what Prince Fredrick identified as "the royal mile." A mile of road that stretches between the kingdom administration buildings to Mengo palace. Along this mile of road each of the 52 clans that make up the Buganda Kingdom has a totem on a plot of land. Each totem represents their clan, such as there is a monkey clan." Prince Fredrick pointed to a small plot of land with a statue of a monkey on it with beautiful trees surrounding it. "Each person in the Kingdom when they say their names, we can tell which clan they are from. It is frowned upon for people to marry from within their own clan, the four fathers knew that DNA should not be mixed within the clans."

As Prince Fredrick was pointing out the plots along the royal mile, I was staring out the window taking in the beauty as I always do. His voice resonated in the background. Each small plot of land had trees, animals of statues on them, they were all beautiful. It was clear that the culture of the Buganda Kingdom respected their environment and Mother Nature.

Sam pulled in a small parking lot. We got out of the car to an entry way that had a statue of a lion on either side. What you would expect the entry way of a royal palace in east Africa to look like. It was quite an amazing sight. There were two gentlemen dressed on uniforms greeted us speaking Luganda, I assumed they were palace guards. After they were done speaking to Prince Fredrick, the big entry way doors opened, as they opened, it revealed Mengo palace. It was not what I had expected. I guess Hollywood movies had put bigger expectations in my mind. Nevertheless, it was still magnificent in it own way.

It was big yellow building, look like it was built in the 1960s. Beautiful with a quite regal feeling to it. The landscape around it was typical of that area. Looks like what you would think the Garden of Eden looked like. The two men directed us to the right into a small building. As I entered, a young lady came forward to say that it was tradition for ladies to wear a dress on the palace grounds. I had dressed for my visit to the palace like I dress in Las Vegas. When Prince Fredrick invited me, he got me. But I understood traditions were necessary to follow. The young lady began to put a very colorful skirt around my waist. When she was done, I felt like a Princess.

The reality of what I was living was beginning to sink in. I was standing next to an African Prince in Uganda, a country in East Africa, a woman with MS, who had survived abuse, and a severe car accident. A little over a year before I left my entire life behind running for safety with just a suitcase. I paused for a moment to take in my reflection in the mirror. I though to myself that I was grateful for my life and how unique and beautiful it had become.

A young man came up to us and introduced himself as our palace guide. His name did not stick in my mind. He was the person that was going to tell me what I wanted to know about Edward Mutesa II. The king that built this palace I was standing in front of with his grandson, Prince Fredrick. Mutesa had lived through much of the same things I had so I was ready to hear his story.

Sam, Fredrick, the palace guide and I walked to the entrance of the palace. Fredrick directed me to sit down with him in on the stairs in front of the palace. We laughed together as we sat for pictures. The kiss earlier was quite a surprise to me, but it was the first time we had been alone together. After we posed for the camera the tour guide stated that we could not go inside certain places in the palace without the King's permission. Which was fine with me, I was there for him to tell me King Mutesa's story.

We began to walk around the palace grounds, the guide pointed out the wall where Mutesa had to jump to his safety. From the inside it did not look that high, but I remembered from the outside, that wall looked like it was a great height. That must have been very frightening for him to run for his life in that way. I understood the feeling of not being able to turn back. Like me, he had no choice. He went to England during his exile. His life story included being with the Queen of England, the Pope, and world leaders. My story was not similar in that way. I did not grow up royalty, my parents were factory workers from West Virginia. I am from a different culture, continent and country. But I could understand what it felt like for him to have to run for his life. One human understanding what another went through because it was the same situation.

We continued to walk past a couple of run-down buildings. There were chickens, and a few children playing in the front. The scenery took a turn from the beauty that surrounded the palace. From bright, beautiful, picturesque landscape to dark, and run down. The palace guide said that these some of the first buildings built there on that property. They were keeping them in their original state. I found it sad and I waved at the little girl playing on the ground outside of one of those little rundown buildings. The guide pointed ahead said that the torture chambers of Idi Admin were just ahead.

Former President of Uganda Idi Admin had made quite an impression on the world. In the United States there was a movie made regarding Iddi Amin; in 2006 his role was portrayed actor Forrest Whittaker. I started to wonder why there was never one made about the first President of Uganda, Edward Mustesa, a King and a decorated military man who was Knighted by the Queen of England. President Mutesa had enemies that were powerful, influential but not nice people. His enemies got the glory and he died in exile in England. His story was the perfect example that the good guy does not always win.

I began to feel cold as we approached the torture chambers built by Idi Amin. A sense of sadness filled my body. Fredrick must have noticed the sadness on my face, he put his arm around me to comfort me. They are chambers that were dug underground, so the physical coldness came from the chambers. The feeling of sadness began when I saw the sign to the right of the entrance of the chambers that states: 'Welcome to the Iddi Amin's Armory that was constructed by the Israeli in the early 1970s but later turned into a torture chamber where thousands of Ugandans lost their lives.'

The palace guide began to tell me the story of what happened in Amin's torture chambers. People who were considered enemies of the state were taken there to be tortured. First, they were put in cars and driven around Kampala so that they would not know where they were located when they got out of the car. On the walls where messages written in blood. With the blood that was coming from their bodies they wrote on the walls to the tell the world what they had experienced. Tears began to fill my eyes at the sight of the bloody messages on the walls.

The chambers are up a little off the floor so that the prisoners were high off the ground. At the bottom was water with electricity running through it. If the prisoners tried to jump, they would land in the water and be electrocuted. Sometimes up to 20 people a day lost their lives here. The sight in front of me was the work of Edward Mutesa's enemies, brutal, evil killers. If you disagreed with them this was your fate. An attitude that the current government agrees with they just do not use these torture chambers anymore to get rid of their enemies.

The tour guide then ended our time at the chambers. I know I was ready to move our tour to lighter subjects. He began to show trees that bear fruit called "Jackfruits." A sorely-needed change in the subject matter. He pointed out "the Kabaka's Lake." It is large manmade lake that was dug by hand in 1886 for King Mwanga. He had it built for an escape route during times of war. The entire place is amazingly beautiful but rooted in a bloody, brutal history.

As we walked the palace grounds the guided ended our tour at the same small building where we started. I changed into the clothing I had arrived in that morning. As I changed my clothes back into "Mother Martha' it still felt like a Princess. As we departed ways Fredrick asked if he could see me again before I left Uganda. I had never though about dating before but when a handsome Prince asks you on a date, you say "yes." Sam and I pulled out of the palace driveway, down the royal mile once again and back on the road to Entebbe where my hotel.

That is when I had to examine out how I felt about men and romantic relationships. Most of my life the men in my life were abusive in some way. My father was an alcoholic, and verbally abusive. I could never do anything right. When he drank, he really bad-mouthed women. After a couple of beers, he would begin to pick on my mother. I learned to stand up to him at an early age. My brother was 13 years older than me, so he was not around much. Then my ex-husband never had anything good to say to me or about me. The men in my life previously left a bad impression on me.

I knew I had learned from those experiences. I knew what I did not want and what I did want in a relationship. I was stronger and wiser because of it all. In fact, I was grateful for it all. Not only was I now strong enough to stand up for myself, but I was strong enough to stand up for others. I felt I was ready to start dating again. Which was good because I had made a date with a Prince.

I am usually a grumpy morning person but that morning I was so excited about my day I jumped out of bed and into the shower at 7 am. Happy John was coming to spend the day with me. We have so much fun together. We both have a sunny disposition, we like to joke and laugh. It is like we have our own language. They do not call us twins because we look alike. I am a short Italian lady with medium brown, curly hair, pale white skin and big blue eyes. People usually comment on the color of my eyes when they first meet me. John is slender built, a little shorter than me, brown eyes, dark skin and a thick mustache. I frequently tease him about his mustache. Our appearance is completely different but the similarities in our personalities got us the nickname "twins."

We spent the day eating at the hotel restaurant and telling jokes. We get loud at times, the receptionist came around the corner because she could hear us through the walls, she politely came into the room and stated to us "you two talking sound like Paula Dean talking to the Queen of England." That did not make us talk lower, in fact we burst out laughing. Since I have an accent from Southeast United States and John English is the "Queen's English," I am sure it probably sounded much different than the conversations they are used to hearing there. It was great day with my friend. Every moment spent with John is a moment I treasure.

Sam called me as John was getting ready to leave the hotel. He was telling me what time he was picking me up in the morning. The next day we were going to the Nile River. Sam informed me that he would be there early, like 6 am. He had been around me enough to know I am a grumpy morning person. He was learning to deal with me accordingly. I will look out the windows and be silent until I am ready to talk.

The next morning Sam picked me up, then drove into Kampala to pick up Geofrey and his friend Musa. We were going to Jinga, Uganda where the source of the Nile River is located. It is about a 3-hour drive, so we all packed a bag of essential items just in case. We stopped for lunch halfway there. They had decided that I should try food from a village on the way. No pizza or Coca-Cola on this trip. It was going to be an authentic Ugandan experience.

We laughed and exchanged stories in the car along the way to the source of the Nile. The time seemed to fly by. Sam interrupted the laughter coming from the back seat, "We are stopping here for lunch," as we pulled up in front of a row of buildings. It was an exceedingly small building that did not even have a door. The entrance was a piece of cloth. After pushing the cloth to the side, I noticed that floors were literally dirt, and there were 4 tables inside. Two tables on the left and two on the right of the entrance. We sat down at the first table to the left. I ask Geofrey to order my food for me as he took the seat to my right. I recognized rice and plantains on the menu, but I did not have any idea what anything else was on the menu.

A lady in a dress with holes in the bottom, looked to be in her 50s took our order and then disappeared behind a door to what I assumed was the kitchen. I wanted to see what the kitchen looked like. What I saw I was not prepared for, the waitress and another young lady, looked like her daughter possibility were the only ones in that room. The stove was an open fire, the younger lady was on her hands and knees scrubbing the floor. The thoughts started to race in my mind. As a nurse my first thought was, please do not get burned by the open flame. But as I looked at the forearms of those ladies, their arms were full of burns. Some looked healed and some looked fresh. I could see that getting burned might have been just a daily part of their lives. My next thought was of the images of kitchens I had seen in Las Vegas. Culture is one thing, but safety is another.

I went back to my table with a great curiosity of what this food would be like. When the food was put in front of me, I looked up to see that everyone at the table was looking at me. I laughed out loud, "Why are you all looking at me? I guess you are looking at my face to see my reaction to it." They were indeed waiting for the American's reaction to Matooke. It is a common dish in East Africa made from plantains of the Great Lake Region. To an American they looked like mashed potatoes. But they sure did not taste like mashed potatoes. My first bite they got the funny face reaction they were looking for, to me it tasted bland. With each taste of each different food on my plate, I asked them what it was I was eating. Besides the Matooke, I loved my first lunch in a Ugandan village.

After our lunch we got back in the car headed to Jinja. I prayed for those ladies working that small restaurant as we left. I prayed for their safety around that open fire. On the drive to Jinja, the scenery turned to sugar cane fields on both sides of the road. Geofrey began to tell me about the resources in Uganda. He told me that coffee was one of the biggest exports. You would think that people would have coffee makers in their homes to enjoy one of their greatest resources. However, it is not true, only 11% of the population have electricity so instant coffee is used frequently. I am not much of a coffee drinker but by that point in my trip I started the habit of making tea in the mornings. The tea there is the best I had ever tasted. I noticed some people put instant coffee in their morning tea as well. Another habit I started on the trip, it surprisingly tasted good to me.

As we entered the source of the Nile, we stopped at the hotel building to freshen up and go to the restroom. On the road to the source, we were stopped at a gate by a man speaking a language I did not recognize. Based on the look on Sam's face, he must have recognized the man. He takes people there frequently for tours, so it was possible. They talked for a few minutes and the man started to point around to everyone in the car. The man had an angry look on his face as he pointed. Sam raised his voice to the man and then handed him money, the guy opened the gate. He must have noticed the sad look on my face because Sam turned his head and said, "Don't worry about it, Martha." I stated back, "I never pay attention to such ignorance." Just like in Dubai, the man had a problem with a white lady being in the presence of African men. None of us paid attention to his ignorance. We drove through the gate to the parking area.

We parked and then had to walk down this steep staircase. I said out loud, "Well if someone is handicapped, they are not visiting the source of the Nile." With having MS, I was having difficulty walking these stairs. Not much stops me, but they were a challenge. I was feeling short of breath by the time we reached the bottom. Musa, a very tall young man that was with us said, "Just take a break Martha, we are in no hurry." I sat for a moment to catch my breath. Then stood up, "Lets go!"

On the walk to the source there were vendors selling paintings and things to help you remember your trip to the Nile. Musa stopped to buy me a keychain with a drum on it. It was sweet; I think he felt sorry for Mother Martha having to stop and rest. Such a kind gesture that I will always remember.

What came into sight I can only describe as "amazing." The first thing on our right was a monument to Gandhi. We stopped to honor him; Gandhi was a great leader in the country of India and in the world. We took many pictures there at that statue. As I looked out on the water, I saw the boats resting, and a man inside one sleeping as he waited for fishermen or tourists to hire him. I thought that would be a great job to have. To sit and relax in this beauty until it was time to go to work.

Sam stated that some of the water is very rapid and that he frequently rafts here. West Virginia is known for white water rafting - in fact, the New River Gorge in southern West Virginia is known world wide for its white-water rafting. We agreed we did not have time that day but on our next trip there we would go rafting together.

We walked through a small zoo that kept animals that are native to that area.. A young girl gave us a short tour. She kept looking at Geofrey like I look at the gelato at the Venetian Hotel in Las Vegas. I recognized that look, and so did Musa, and Sam. But Geofrey was clueless, as she was walking us through showing us the different animals. When we left that area, we all began to tease him. I said "Geofrey she could not have been more obvious. Maybe if she threw herself on you that would have given you a clue." We all laughed at Geofrey's naivety.

The next thing we saw was a traditional hut complete with all the things used for daily life without electricity. Once again, I was fascinated and shocked at the same time. The same thoughts going through my mind as when I saw the ladies cooking in the kitchen with the open fire. I was impressed by the genius of it and saddened by seeing the burns on the arms of those ladies in that village restaurant. We decided to get some dinner before ending back to Entebbe. First we wanted one last look at the source.

As we were looking out from the shore, as I turned my head to the right, I then heard a big splash. Sam and I look down to see Geofrey underwater being pulled by the current holding his cellphone up out of the water as if to say, "Save the cell phone." I threw down my purse immediately to prepare to get into the water to save him. My heart sunk as I ran toward the water. Sam was right behind me. We got to the edge of the swift water to see Geofrey fighting to make it to shore. Swinging his arms from side to side. His arm got close enough for us to reach him. We pulled him out of the water onto the rocky shore. Geofrey let out a big cough and water came out of his mouth. Sam and I looked at each other with relief and then I looked at Geofrey in a way a mother does before she is about to correct their child. "You almost gave me a heart attack Geofrey! How can you worry about that cell phone? We can replace a cell phone but not you!" After I got my anger out, I then began to hug him. Thankful that he was safe. Sam is such a patience man. He never said a word as he was drying himself off with an extra shirt that he had brought with him. We all agreed that Geofrey falling in the Nile River was enough drama for the day, so we decided to drive back to Entebbe that evening. It was a long drive, but I enjoyed watching the sunset in backdrop of the Ugandan sugar cane fields.

The next day I spent getting ready for my date with Prince Fredrick. I was a bit nervous because it was my first date since I left my long term yet abusive marriage. I started to come to terms with how I felt about men. I had healed so much since I left with that suitcase just a year before. Just a few years before I was a broken and battered woman. I had little self-esteem. Has I sat there in my hotel room putting on make-up for my date with a very handsome

African Prince, I realized that I had found my-self. I do not like clichés, but I had to admit this one was indeed true. I had lost everything including my face in the car accident, and now I had found myself.

A friend in Las Vegas made the comment that I had a heart of gold, the courage of a lion and a sassy mouth. Well one thing is for sure, I could stand up for myself. I was brave enough to leave with just that suitcase without knowing where I was going. I had the courage to start the charitable foundations, and to fly across the planet by myself. Now I had the courage to go out on a date for the first time in a long time. I guess if you are going to get your grove back, going out with a handsome Prince was a great way to do that.

I got ready and went down to the reception area of the hotel at dinner time to met Prince Fredrick. When he showed up, he was dressed in a suit and tie. Very handsome slender man, the very image of his grandfather. "Hello Martha how are you doing?" he said with a big smile so bright it could have light up the room. "I am fine Fredrick" me trying to match his big smile. We walked to the dinning area of the hotel. I picked it because it was close to my hotel room. I still had some trust issues with men, and I figured if he turned out to be a creep, I could ask him to leave and just go back up to my hotel room. Just because someone has a fancy title or even royal DNA that does not make them a nice person. I was about to find out if Prince Fredrick lived up to his title of Prince.

He pulled out my chair at the table of the dinning area then sat right next to me. We exchanged pleasantries and then we looked at the menu. We began to compare American food with Ugandan food. I pulled out a copy of my book 'Lead with your Heart' then stated, "I thought I would sign a copy of my book for you. It is my life story up until now." Fredrick looked over with a surprised look on his face "So dear Martha, you are putting it out there first off." "My story is out there for anyone to read. I have nothing to hide. What you see is what you get." I stated bluntly.

"Well good then, do you know what you want to have for dinner?" I closed my menu and stated I will have the fish and French fries. I forgot, here they are called chips. In the US, what we call chips are very thin crispy potato slices. As the waitress was taking the menus, Fredrick leaned forward and put his hand on mine. "Enough about food. Tell me more about you." I found this move to be a bit forward, but I understood he was a man of power and used to getting what he wanted.

I looked at our hands touching on the table then looked up at Fredrick's face looking directly in my eyes. I thought to myself, I recognize that look, that is how I look at the gelato at the Venetian Hotel back in Las Vegas. With a look of embarrassment on my face I stuttered, "Hmm, what would you like to know?" Fredrick said with that amazing smile, "Whatever you feel comfortable telling me." Just then he began to slowly lean it to kiss me. It was slow and gentle. Not rushed like before a few days ago at the palace. This time we were not interrupted.

That kiss broke the tension between us. After that, my shoulders began to relax, we began to talk about our lives, our likes and dislikes. Just as any other first date. Our food came, we laughed, and enjoyed each other's company until the restaurant was ready to close for the night. The waitress came around to say that they were closing for the night in an hour. After all I was used to Las Vegas where nothing closes, I apologized for the inconvenience. The young lady stated, "It is fine, we are glad you enjoyed your dinner." We paid the bill, then Fredrick stated he would call for a car home but first he was going to walk me to my hotel room before returning to Kampala.

It had been a long time since I was single and was on a first date. I had never been on a date with an African Prince. As we stood at my hotel door I felt like an awkward teenager. I kept thinking "What is the proper etiquette? Do I invite him in? What are the cultural norms here?" My mind was filled with anxiety and it showed on the outside. I awkwardly took out my keys to my hotel room from my purse and then they fell in the floor. Fredrick being a gentleman picked them up for me. I said, "Thank you as I opened the door." I looked at him while I was turning the key, the thought in my mind were, "He isn't leaving. Why is he still standing here?"

Even an awkward teenager could answer that question. It was basic human nature and obvious as to why he was still standing there. However, the anxiety would not allow me to see it. I asked him, "Would you like to come inside for a night cap, as you know I do not drink alcohol, but I do have some water and Coca-Cola." Fredrick said with a smile, "Sure" as he entered the room.

He quickly made himself at home in the room. Sitting on the side of the bed. Which made me more uncomfortable. I said, "I will get that water for you." I came back with that water and as he reached for the bottle of water, he grabbed me and pulled me into the bed. He was a man of power and he was going to get what he wanted.

The next morning, I woke up in Entebbe, Uganda at Frontiers Hotel in my bed with a tall dark and handsome Prince in the bed beside me. As I opened my eyes to see him sleeping next to me, it was almost like a dream. I just kept thinking, "How on Earth did this happen?" I still had some self-esteem issues left from the past. But what a great way to get back into dating then to spend the night with a handsome African Prince.

As Prince Fredrick rose from the bed he said, "Good morning honey pie." I just looked at him as if to say, "Who is he talking to?" He said "I like the way you talk, the accent and how you call people darlin' and doll. I thought my nickname for you should be honey pie." I laughed "Honey pie it is then." We got dressed and walked back to the restaurant for break-fast. Fredrick pulled out his cell phone to call for a car home for two hours later. He said he had a meeting to attend that morning and he could not get late for it. We had a lovely break-fast, we said goodbye a couple of hours later.

I went back to my hotel room to get ready for dinner that evening. Sam was picking me up to meet Zaake Francis Butebi. The parliament member that I had watched being hit in the head by a chair on television over a year ago when I was living in Blaine, Minnesota with Ivan and Joe.

Shortly after being assaulted by a chair on the floor of parliament in Uganda, Zaake was kid-napped and tortured by the President's army. From my living room in Las Vegas, I watched a YouTube video of him recounting that experi-ence. I reached out to him out of sympathy. If you look through out history, people who were brave enough to step forward, to make a stand for the rights of others were not treated well. The forward thinkers, and change makers are frequently beaten, tortured and jailed. People such as MLK, Jr, Nelson Mandela, and Gandhi just to name a few.

A President is no longer a president of country when they forget that they are in office to serve the people. They become dictators when they change the laws of the land to benefit themselves. Control the people using fear becomes their mode of operation. Zaake was kidnapped because he was of the opposing political party in Uganda called People Power Party.

The People Power Movement is led by Bobi Wine. Robert Kyagulanyi Ssentmu, his stage name, Bobi Wine, gained his influence and popularity through being a popular musician. Zaake Francis and Bobi Wine were both parliament members, and leadership of the People Power Movement. I had never met or spoken to Bobi Wine, but I reached out to Zaake many times in the previous year and struck up a friendship with him.

To an American, kidnapping and torture seem like we are talking about something that happened in the past, like events from the middle ages. Unfortunately, in Uganda it was common. Fear is how dictators control people. Once people are living in controlled living in fear, then it easier to take from them. Leaving the general population so suppressed that they cannot rise, and they are stuck in the mentality, and the poor economic conditions.

Geofrey had been kidnapped and tortured the summer of 2018 when I was in Minnesota living with Ivan and Joe. I did everything I could to save him all the way from Ivan and Joe's living room in Minnesota, over 7,000 miles away from where he was in Uganda. After all, he and his brother had saved my life. It is a true act of love when you help another when you are also in a time of need. Geofrey still has emotional and physical affects from the torture. I hope some day he can heal from them both. It is not my place to tell you about what he lived through that summer, that is Geofrey's story to tell. Knowing what happened to Geofrey made me more sympathetic to what Zaake had lived through.

Sam picked me up in the reception area of the hotel as always. I think he was a little excited about this trip. He was getting to meet Zaake Francis too. Zaake was gaining a lot of popularity in Uganda. We were meeting him at Pope Paul International Hotel in Kampala. The nicer part of town, across the street from the dinning area you can see one of palaces of Prince Fredrick's Uncle, King Ronald Mutebi.

Our drive through Kampala had become one of my favorite things to do. Difficult to imagine that a woman who lives in a famous place like Las Vegas could fall in love with a place that is the complete opposite. I think it is the kindness of the people and the culture there that I fell in love with. They have a barbaric government, but the people of Uganda have beautiful kind hearts. When my life was in danger my Ugandan family had my back. For that I will always be grateful for them.

Compared to Las Vegas hotels, Pope Paul International Hotel was average on the inside. African style décor, but classy. Sam and I went toward the bar and sat at a table. We ordered food while we waited for Zaake to arrive. I ordered a hamburger and Sam ordered something that looked like African food trying to be American food. Just as we were finishing our dinner, Zaake came around the corner of the bar. My first thought was, he is much more attractive in person. He is a man of average height, round face, body is built round, a big, beautiful smile with a small dimple on the side.

Zaake approached the table and shook our hands and introduced himself to us. He suggested we move outside. Since the weather was beautiful, we agreed. I never miss out on enjoying the beauty of Uganda. We sat at a table in which King Mutebi's palace could be seen behind us. Sam sat across from us and Zaake sat on the same side of the table. As I looked behind me, I remembered what had happened the night before, I woke up in bed next to King Mutebi's nephew. At that moment I thought to myself, this is what my life has become as Mother Martha of Uganda. It felt quite amazing and uniquely ridiculous as well.

We ordered more food and drinks to settle in to talk to Zaake about whatever he felt comfortable with telling us. Just like any other time with friends we were getting to know each other, laughing and eating. Since I am passionate about helping children, Zaake showed me videos of the living conditions of some children in the Mityana Municipality in which he represents as a member of parliament. The living conditions were worse than anything I had seen. A sense of sadness came over me for those children, but I could sense the determination in his voice to make a difference.

An hour later a man dressed in uniform approached the table from my right side. It did not startle me, after all there when you go to the ATM in Uganda are armed guards on both sides of you with AK-47s. It is common to see uniformed officers with weapons walking around especially in downtown Kampala. The man walked behind me and then to the left side of Zaake. I looked over at Sam, his smile turned to a look of concern. It was obviously that the man approaching the table was not one the good guys.

The gentleman stood there for a few moments in silence. By then we all had a look on concern on our faces. I was aware that sitting next to Zaake in Uganda was a risk. It was like if we were sitting next to Mandela in South Africa during the time when the apartheid was a system was ruling. The man spoke to Zaake then put his hand out in a gesture to shake his hand. The looks of concern on our faces then turned to surprise, we thought the man was coming to make trouble. Instead, he was coming to make peace. Zaake then shook his hand. The gentleman identified himself as secret service agent of the Vice President of Uganda. He then pointed to the bar where a man was sitting having a drink. He did not say tell us who he was pointing to, but I assumed that was Edward Seekandi, the Vice President of Uganda.

The secret service officer said to Zaake, "We only bother you because we are ordered to do so. I urge you to continue on." Then he quietly told us all to have a good night. The heavy tension I was feeling began to release. I could see a look of relief on Sam's face. I let out an awkward laugh, to break the tension. I am known to tell jokes during inappropriate times like these. As the man walked away, I said out loud, "Well I do not blame him for having a drink at the bar after work, if my boss was a dictator, I would want to have a drink after work too." Sam and Zaake began to laugh out loud which broke the tension. I then said, "I am from Las Vegas we pay no mind to famous people drinking at bars. If he would not have pointed out the Vice President sitting there, I would have not known who he was." Although we were laughing, I knew then why Zaake wanted to us to eat outside. His enemies were close by, inside the hotel. Being outside where there were a little more people provided a little more safety.

About an hour after that encounter, Zaake decided to call it a night and return to his family. I needed to get back to my hotel to prepare to fly out of Entebbe the next morning. It had been an amazing visit, leaving there was like leaving my home. Nevertheless, knew as I was hugging Zaake good-bye and getting into Sam's car that this was only the beginning of my adventures in Uganda. A place I now considered my second home.

The next morning Sam and John drove me to the airport. John was sitting next to in the back seat with me. Each time I looked over at him he seemed to be pouting, I guess because I was leaving Uganda. They walked me as far as they could toward the boarding gate. I hugged Sam and then John. John said, "Where are you going next my twin?" "Milan, Italy" I said with excitement. He stated, "Why there?" I said, "Why else John? For the pizza, of course!"

I boarded the plane from Entebbe International Airport with the destination of Milan, Italy. As I sit on the plane thought about my trip so far start running through my mind. I was not the same I women I was when I left Charleston, West Virginia with that suitcase just a few years earlier, I do not even think I was the same woman I was that left Las Vegas a few weeks earlier. I had learned so much about myself and about the world. Now I was going to Italy. I was raised in Northern West Virginian where many immigrants had settled from Italy. I was raised in a mixture of Italian and American culture, and this was the origin of my family. I was excited to enjoy my two favorite things while visiting there, pizza and Coca-Cola.

We landed in Milan 11 hours later. It was late in the evening. I walked out into the tarmac to the beautiful landscape of Milan. When I booked this flight, I did not know it was fashion week in Milan. The rush of people coming in from all over, was exciting. I was dressed in comfortable clothes because of the long flight. I love the clothes, and the entire fashion scene. Because I had come from an area where it is possible to be exposed to Ebola I was pulled to the side for extra screening. I did not blame them for doing it. People were coming here from all over to show off their designs and they could not risk anyone bringing in Ebola.

After getting screened and grabbing my suitcase I went to the front of the airport and googled pizza near me. I was so excited to look down at my phone to see I was looking to find pizza in Italy. I was not staying long, so I had to get busy on the things I wanted to do in this one day stop. I got a ride to take me to the pizza place first, then for a short drive to take in the beauty of Milan. I grew up in Italian American culture, so my Italian was simply good enough to get by. Once again, I found myself looking out the window of the backseat of a car. I did not know anyone in Milan, Italy, it was just me seeing the sights and trying the food on a one day stop. It was something else I could mark off that list I made back in Minnesota just a little over a year ago. Milan did not disappoint. The food was everything I dreamed it would be.

Next stop Paris, France to see the Eiffel Tower. We get these romantic thoughts in our minds about what seeing Paris might be like. Those thoughts filled my mind as the plane descended into Charles de Gaulle airport. The pilot announced that it was 30 degrees in Paris today. I knew that was in Celsius, all I knew was that it was going to be cold when I landed in Paris. I made sure I had Joe's phone number in my phone easily accessible because being from Rwanda he spoke French, but I would use that only if necessary. From my travels I have learned you can find someone that speaks English just about anywhere you go.

After getting my suitcase, I remember getting my phone out to take a video. For some reason, the shops inside Charles de Gaulle airport seemed fancy to me for being inside an airport. In the United States we have shops inside the international boarding flight areas, but the shops there seemed to be more upscale.

To my surprised everything I wanted to see while in Paris, I could see in one long day. The Eiffel Tower, and the Louvre Museum were the two that were on my list. The Mona Lisa, an iconic painting. A copy hung in a few of my grade school classrooms as a child. No way I was going to try drive here either. The narrow streets, the steering wheel on the right side and driving on the left side of the road was a combination I was not used to. My driving skills is one of the things my friends in Uganda tease me about, especially Francis. I was not about to test those skills during any part of this trip.

The most beautiful skies and sunsets I have ever seen were during my brief stop in Paris. It might have more romantic if that Prince was at my side. But alone it was amazing as well. Ordering food was a little challenging being unfamiliar with the language and the food. I had seen the tower at the Paris Hotel in Las Vegas and eaten at the restaurant there, but I knew that was Americanized French food. It is a beautiful place, rich in history, peaceful environment full of charm. After just two days there it was time to end my trip and go back to Las Vegas.

I had been away from Las Vegas for almost 3 weeks, but it felt like entirely new experience coming back. I had met so many new friends, I had spent time with friends, and possibly started a new romance. Time would reveal the fate of relationship between Prince Fredrick and me. After all there was 10,000 miles between us. It was possible I was just another conquest to the single young Prince. But I am not complaining it was a great way to get my grove back.

CHAPTER 7:

Transformation

The flight back to Las Vegas was an entire day in the air. I love to fly but the long flight takes a toll on my body having Multiple Sclerosis and many replacement parts. When I landed at Mc-Carran International Airport, I took a picture of the small, Welcome to Las Vegas sign. It was a great trip, but I was happy to be home. The famous Elvis song Viva Las Vegas rang in my head as my Uber driver pulled up to the front door of my apartment.

I had planned to rest for a few days before returning to work. I crashed into my King size bed when I arrived exhausted yet happy. After a few hours of rest, I woke up feeling feverish and my lungs felt tight. I looked in the mirror and thought to myself, I took the malaria medication as directed. I cannot have malaria. Malaria prevention should be taken 3 days before entering the malaria zone every day while in it and then a days after leaving the malaria zone. I had slept under the net the hotel provided. I was trying to convince myself that this was not malaria and I went back to bed.

After just a few minutes the room began to spin, and my fever spiked. It was time to admit that this was malaria. I thought the incubation period was over for malaria to come on, but I was wrong. My few days of rest turned into much longer. Having MS there was a concern that the malaria would take the MS out of remission, but it did not and after a week I returned to work at the hospital. Having malaria made me have more sympathy for the people I met in Uganda that told me they have had malaria up to 17 or 18 times in their lives. Those people were young people, they will probably have it many more times in their lifetimes.

During that time, I had time to think about how I was going to help Uncle Joseph at Bulamu Children's Village. The foundation was started, and my book was out. The book had minimal success, but it was a start. I started a website and did some calling local businesses for sponsors.

Being in a big city alone was a challenge plus I had taken on such a big life's purpose. But I was up for the challenge. Prince Fredrick and I ended our relationship, moving to just being friends. I am not complaining, what a great way to get my groove back with a handsome African Prince. I decided it was time for a social life and time to get start building Mother Martha Family Foundation.

Happy John Buganda and I talked every day. We would talk through FaceTime or WhatsApp when it was morning for me and it was nighttime for him, so he would put his son to bed before talking to me. He would never wear a shirt, was not sure if it were a hint or he was just preparing for bed. I teased him by calling him 'shirtless John.' Then say to him, "Put a shirt on John all I can see on the screen is chest hair." My connection with my twin never decreased because of the distance between us. I never asked him about Hilton's mother, it is truly none of my business. However, all I knew was that she was not in his life. The connection with "my twin' remained intact and strong as ever. In time he began to wear a shirt more frequently.

A friend from the east coast moved from Florida to Las Vegas to be near her son. I remember texting her as she landed at the airport, Kelly when you get settled, we need to get together. After a couple of weeks, she called me. We made plans to go to the Mirage Hotel at the Siegfried and Roy's Secret garden and Dolphin Habitat. We both share a love of animals. Kelly had worked for the EPA in Florida for most of her career her work involved helping to protect marine life. We hit it off immediately, besties at first sight. Now I had my Las Vegas bestie and my twin, John my bestie in Uganda. A best friend in each of the places I loved the most. Which lead me to start saying, my heart is always split between Las Vegas and Uganda.

I called the foundation that was created in Nevada, Mother Martha Family Foundation because of the new family I had created all over the world after leaving with that suitcase. Most of my new family being in Las Vegas and Uganda. One family coming together for a common cause. It was not an instant success by any means. Anything worth having does not come easily. In fact, the bigger the goal the more difficult the road. I knew I could do it, in my life I had built my own house with my own hands. I had overcome a car accident in which no one thought I would. I had lived much of what you would call a normal life living with Multiple Sclerosis since 2008. I had not only survived living in abuse but thrived after walking away from my life with just a suitcase. I had now "found myself." The butterfly was free from its cocoon. 'Mother Martha' was ready to build her foundation in order to help the children of Bulamu Children's Village.

I then began my adventure exploring Las Vegas. I enjoyed the journey my friends. I began to explore and enjoy everything that makes Las Vegas the iconic place that it is. The Venetian Hotel became my favorite spot. When there was something on my mind the porch of the Venetian Hotel could soothe me right away. The memories of my grandparents and their love came flooding back in the Venice style architecture. The gondola rides and the gondoliers singing brought back memories of my grandmother singing in the kitchen as she made homemade pasta. Every time it takes me back to when I felt loved as a child.

Pizza and Coca-Cola were always present in my life. I found my favorite place in Boulder City, Nevada. A small town just outside of Las Vegas know to be the home of the Hoover Damn. Tony's Pizza the typical Italian pizza shop, family owned. Grandmother, grandson and daughter can always be found behind the counter to greet you with a smile. I love to go to the Lake Mead overlook to gauze out at its beautiful shoreline. It is not Lake Victoria but just as impressive in its own way.

Through my friendships especially with my male friends, I learned a lot about relationships and myself. I had learned from my previous relationships what I wanted and what I did not want. I realized that I had built a wall around myself in a sense. Not letting in many people. Not really showing pictures of myself. I told myself I built this wall to protect myself from my ex coming back around to hurt me. But what it did was keep others from coming in. A defense mechanism due to the trauma from the abuse. I gave it the excuse that I was protecting myself but that threat that was no longer there.

Showing people how I perceived the world around me became something I did everyday through my writings and social media. I was sharing with the world what I had learned from my journey as my way of "paying it forward." I thought if I shared the wisdom and knowledge that I learned that it might help someone else along the way. Within my life's experiences, there was some part of it others could relate to or had experienced in their lives. Someone out there reading my words as been in an abusive relationship, face health issues, been in a car accident or been betrayed by those they loved.

I had not arrived at the destination, or the goal I had set for myself, but I had enjoyed the journey along the way. Learned a few things about life and love. Through sharing those words of wisdom, I hoped it would help someone else along the way.

I kept in touch with Prince Fredrick. After my tour of Mengo palace, I voiced my interest in writing a book about his grandfather, Edward Mutesa II. I felt such a connection to him because of the similarities in our stories. People knew about his enemies but not about how his bravery had changed a country. A movie had made about his enemy former President Idi Amin called 'The last King of Scotland' in which actor Forest Whitaker portrayed the role of Amin. I stood in the torture chambers that Amin built at Mengo palace wondering why Mutesa's side of the story had never been told. The "bad" guys seem to get more attention than the heroes at times.

Fredrick had told me that there was a Prince from the Buganda kingdom living in Los Angeles that is a writer, that I should give him a call. Maybe we could collaborate on a book about his grandfather. When he mentioned his name,

Prince Gerald Mwanga, I remembered having a brief conversation with him in the past, so I thought giving him a call was a good idea.

A few days later I called him as I was cooking dinner, my friend Kelly was waiting patiently in the kitchen of my apartment. Turned out he was writing a book about the history of the Buganda Kingdom that was near completion. He invited me to come see in Los Angeles. I accepted the invitation and said I would call back to set up the details. As dinner was complete, Kelly began to tease me about calling a Prince. I assured her that his was business not funny business.

Two weeks later I landed at Los Angeles International Airport to meet Prince Gerald. He is a descendant of King Mwanga who was the grandfather of Edward Mutesa. As a writer he had researched the history of his kingdom well. He was qualified to write about Mutesa with me. Prince Gerald was waiting for me at the passenger picked me up at LAX. When our eyes connected, I noticed he had a surprised looked on his face. He said "Martha?" as if he was not sure if it was me. "Look at you," he stated with a smile. I have been told in the past that I am better looking in person then in pictures. I thought the same thing about Zaake when I met him. I think pictures are just a "snapshot" of a person and we cannot take in their full essence until we are in their presence. I was not sure how I should take Prince

Gerald's reaction to me, but it was clear that he was attracted to me.

We decided to have lunch to talk about writing and to get to know each other. We chose a place on Sunset Boulevard. We hit it off quickly. He showed me the draft of his book, 'A Long Walk to Freedom.' One chapter in it focused on Mutesa. Prince Gerald told me about his life in Uganda as a doctor. I told him some of my experience being a nurse in the United States. We had two things in common, both of us were writers and we had experience working in hospitals. We talked for a couple of hours, time seemed to fly by, I started to notice the waitress look over at our table with a look of frustration. Probably wondering when we going to leave so she could get new customers at her table. We paid the bill, and I ordered an Uber to pick me up. I had a meeting to attend while I was there in West Hollywood and then I was going to check into my hotel. We agreed that we would meet up later for dinner.

I love the nostalgia of everything in Hollywood. The Hollywood walk of fame, the studios, and the movie memorabilia. Seeing a prop from a movie takes me back to when I first watched that movie. Memories begin to flood my mind of what my life was like then or even what was going on in the world at that time. Great stories captivate our minds, we relate to the characters on screen from experiences in our own lives. Walking through the gate of paramount pictures reminds me of the movie 'Sunset Boulevard.' I have to say the famous line from that movie, out loud or just in my mind, "I am ready for my close-up, Mr. De-Mille." Movies have a way of capturing life's moments, entertain us, make us laugh or make us cry. We get engrossed in the adventure of the characters giving us a brief break from our daily lives.

After the meeting I met Prince Gerald at Lucy's El Adobe Café, Mexican restaurant on Melrose Ave across the street from Paramount Studios. A landmark restaurant in Hollywood, the walls lined with signed autographed pictures from movie stars, politicians, and musicians. Small family-owned restaurant that made me feel at home. Based on the number signed autographed pictures on the walls, many other people felt the same way while being there.

Gerald is a slender built man, strong silent type, much like Geofrey, very matter of fact in his conversations. That I liked about him, no beating around the bush, he speaks out about how he sees things. I have two modes, serious which can be seen in my writing, or sassy and humorous. I switch between the two quickly when I need to. We decided we would write something together and that we had started a friendship. We had laughed and talked all evening, at thirty minutes before closing time, I look at the time on my cellphone and then looked at Prince Gerald, "We had better get going, it is almost closing time, and they might throw us out of here."

He walked me to my hotel room just down the block. I remembered the last time an African Prince from the Buganda Kingdom walked me home. Prince Fredrick had been going to get to what he wanted that night. With every step during the two-block walk from Lucy's El Café to my hotel room, I was wondering if Prince Gerald was going to be the same way. It was a beautiful night out, typical California weather. As we entered the hotel he walked me up the stairs, and as I opened the door Prince Gerald surprised me, but he was the perfect gentleman. He said good-bye with a soft kiss to the lips. Although he had not made any big bold moves, it was clear he wanted more than friendship.

A few weeks later Prince Gerald flew to Las Vegas to see me. Knowing that he was a conservative guy and a bit about his culture, I was anticipating that he might be a little shocked by Las Vegas. He was coming to exchange ideas about a possible book about Mutesa. I picked him up at the airport and he planned to stay at my apartment.

That evening I decided to take him to see all the iconic sights of Las Vegas I that I could fit in one night. Caesar's palace, the Bellagio fountains, the volcano at the Mirage, and my favorite the Venetian Hotel. I enjoyed the reaction on his face just from the sights of the beautiful buildings of Vegas. It is all over the top, which I love.

The way women dress in Vegas was shocking to him at first sight. A lady walked by in was a very reliving two-piece bathing suit with a see-through wrap around her. He stopped in his tracks looked at me and said, "Oh my, did you see that black American she was almost naked." Seemed like an over exaggerated reaction to me, I broke out in laughter. I then realized I was living the movie 'Coming to America,' the movie about an African Prince that comes to the United States the first time and experiences culture shock. Prince Gerald was Eddie Murphy's character. I did a lot of explaining things to him that evening. I enjoyed watching the look of awe on his face. It was a comical yet wonderful evening.

We spend the next day going through writings, and me learning about the history of his kingdom. I got to tour Mengo palace but the only history I had learned was around the story of Mutesa's exile and his enemies such as Idi Amin. Not the history of all the Kings, Queens or culture. I had the same look of awe on my face while learning about the history of his kingdom as he did while touring the Las Vegas strip just a few days earlier.

I never thought about a romantic relationship with him. Our personalities being so different. Differences in culture or race never entered my mind as something that might affect us being in a romantic relationship. But something happened I never expected as we were looking over our writings and sharing ideas. As we were eating, talking and laughing we began to sit closer and closer to each other. Next thing I knew, we passionately kissing each other. Which lead to our clothes ending up on the bedroom floor.

That was the beginning of the first relationship that I had after leaving the abusive marriage. I still had the wall around me that I had built. However, I was beginning to tear down that wall little by little. The two of us started going back and forth between Las Vegas and Los Angeles to spend time together.

In the ways we were alike, we really connected. The writing and understanding of our experiences working in the hospital. His background is surgery with performing C-sections and delivering babies was what he loved most. That was never my passion in nursing. I always loved to float between the disciplines but rarely working with babies. Gerald would cook for me, I loved it when he cooked chicken or any foods from Uganda. Living single for a while I had given up on being domestic. He grounded me in many ways.

I was wiser to what I wanted and what I did not want in a relationship. He had gotten out of a relationship around the same time I did, he has a son from that relationship. The relationship got serious enough that I met his family for dinner in Los Angeles. I thought maybe we might be ready for something more serious.

After a few months he ended up staying in California with no talks of visiting me in Las Vegas. I began to be busier with work in Las Vegas. We sort of drifted apart. I do not regret our time together. Just the opposite. We are still close friends, and it was a great learning experience for me. I will be there to support my friend however I can in his writing career. I love Prince Gerald still but in a different way, I hold great respect for him as person and a doctor. I will always hold great respect of the Buganda Kingdom. In the future, I will revisit the idea of writing a book about Edward Mutesa II.

My book 'Lead with your heart' was out there and people were reading it. A friend of a friend read my book and texted me on day. That text read: I think you are an incredibly strong woman. Your book inspired me. Her name is Karen and her text impressed me. It turned out we had many mutual friends together and that started a great connection between us.

My mother and I had not spoken once since 2015. I called her to make amends after living in Las Vegas for a while. I thought she might be relieved to know that I am still alive. Maybe we could have a reunion. After all, if your child just walks away from their life and you finally know what happened to them, it will give a sense of closure or relief. That was not the reaction that I received when I called my mother that I was alive and well. Expectations usually do lead to disappointment. When I told her who I was she immediately said, "I thought you were in California, you know you could have left him sooner." She then informed me that my father was ill and that she was taking care of him. That my brother had to step up and help take care of him.

It was not the response I thought I would get. No, "I am glad you are alive." No, "we have been worried for 5 years." I got, "You could have left him sooner." It was a reminder to not look back. The non-compassion that I had experienced in West Virginia was in the past and that is where I knew I needed to leave it.

That is where a new Mother figure came into my life. Auntie Karen is the nickname that she received from me. She lives on the east coast, the state of Virginia. He has 3 grown children, two sons and a daughter. Her daughter an emergency room doctor. She had been married for a long time and they are both retired. After a couple of weeks being adopted to Mother Martha

Family, she began to sponsor two young men at Bulamu Children's Village. The children have gotten so much joy from her, she then had a new purpose in life. Suddenly our family grew.

The end of the year 2019 brought on something no one on Earth was prepared for, Covid-19. Now I do not think anyone on this planet can remember a time when we did not know the word Covid-19. The words 'social distancing' is ingrained in our brains. Wearing face masks in public have unfortunately become a part of our daily lives. Everyone's life on the planet has been affected in some way by the Corona Virus.

Being a nurse during a pandemic is something that I can only describe as a nightmare. I have been a nurse for some time, but no amount of training could prepare a person's heart and mind for what happened in the year 2020. I worked as a float nurse in health system of three hospitals. I like being a float nurse because routine bores me. I like going to different hospitals and different units every day. I continue to learn that way, I meet new people, plus I do not get involved in the politics of one place. The gossip, people starting dramas, and talking about people's love lives, are the most boring things to me. If people try to tell me any gossip, I set boundaries with them. To me it is a waste of time. I do not care about who is doing what after work, who is dating who, or who does not like whom.

People started coming to the hospital complaining with what they described as 'flu like' symptoms to hours later intubating them or worse, knowing them for a few hours then watching them die. People could not say goodbye to their loved ones. There were people married for 40 to 50 years who said goodbye by FaceTime to their life partners. Then they could not have a proper burial for their loved ones.

Wearing the protective gear over my face after I had the reconstruction surgeries on my face was difficult but necessary. Nevertheless, no matter how much you protect yourself, you are still at risk. Co-workers, nurses and doctors started to get sick, including me. I was sick with the very virus I was helping fight, like many other of my colleges. As healthcare providers we put ourselves at risk to care for others. Respiratory therapist, nurses, doctors, nursing assistance, paramedics, lab technicians, and housekeeping, it takes many people to keep a hospital running properly. I will always be proud of my profession, my co-workers and all the front-line workers for how they stepped up to handle something no one was prepared for in 2020.

I was leaving my shift one evening at a nursing unit that did not have any Covid patients. In the elevator, a nurse looked at me, "Martha you should go to the ER, you do not look well." Being a nurse is something that you cannot turn off. It is something you are, not something you do. It was early on when all the talk about it had just started, so I just thought that I was run down, tired from all the shifts I had been working. I did not go to the ER, I went home, took a shower and then went to bed.

I was lying in my bed when a little after midnight I started to feel warm all over, and my lungs felt tight. It felt much like when I had malaria after I returned from Uganda. Just like with the malaria, I was concerned about MS. I have Relapsing Remitting Multiple Sclerosis which means if it is in remission, I do not have any new symptoms. Where the lesions are on the brain determines what symptoms are experienced. I then took myself to the emergency room as my fellow nurse had recommended that I do that previous evening.

Kelly was my only support; she did the best she could to help me as I recovered. Joe being my hero for the second time in my life, took some time off from his job in Minnesota to come stay for me for a few days. I did not realize what a good friend he was going to be in my life when I met him in the doorway of his apartment in Blaine, Minnesota, back in 2018. Not only is Joe the perfect vision of dark, tall and handsome, he is a good man. He along with other men that came into my life after I left with that suitcase, showed me that there are good men in this world. Previously, the men in my life had left a bad impression on me.

For me, having Covid-19 felt like malaria but the symptoms were much more severe. Not being able to breath, to feel like your lungs are being squeezed, is a frightening feeling. You are laboring for every breath. Just going to the bathroom exhausted me. It was four days before I could shower on my own. Eating was difficult; even if I felt hungry, I could not eat because I was struggling to breathe. But each day I improved. I was thankful that I did not get sick enough to be put on a ventilator or worse. I recovered well, and the MS stayed in remission to my surprise. My body had been through so much in the past, but just like those times, this was not my exit out of this world.

I went through many different emotions during that time. Especially when I started to lose co-workers and friends to Covid-19. After going through all the stages of grief, I concluded, I still had my life and I still had a goal to accomplish. With a heart full of gratitude, I went back to working as a nurse. Each time I have been a patient, over all it helped me to be a better nurse. Once you have lived something then you can understand it.

The year 2020 taught me great lessons, the biggest one: gratitude. To be grateful for the little things. I started to count my blessing as I got up the mornings, I found that gratitude brings joy.

I was missing those free-range chickens in Uganda when a dozen of eggs went to seven dollars a dozen. It learned from seeing people in the hoarding supplies that adversity builds character, but it also reveals character. We saw great acts of kindness. We also saw violence; people being divided more than ever. Many issues came to light in 2020, usually when issues come "to light" in the world it is because people are no longer willing to tolerate them.

For the first time in history, one single event effected the entire world. Now whether you believe in conspiracy theories or not, that statement is true. Every person on the planet Earth's daily lives were affected somehow. That should be proof enough for people to realize that we are connected. Treating each other well can only benefit everyone. We do not have to agree in order to love on another. The story of good versus evil is a story as old as time. Unfortunately, it seems that the bad guys have been in control of the world for quite a while. I am hoping that recent events will "wake" people up to the fact that we must start treating each other with a little more kindness and respect.

Mother Martha Family Foundation was still on a mission to help give back to the children of Bulamu. Due to economic status of the entire world that was put on hold. If people do not have jobs and cannot support themselves, they cannot help others. Nevertheless, the pandemic, nor the conditions of the world could not stop my passion for helping those children.

After all, if Joseph Lubega had not instilled good morals and values in Ivan and Geofrey at Bulamu, I would not be on Earth. I felt it was important to help that continue to bless the world. What he was doing in Kampala, Uganda had saved the life of nurse in West Virginia, but it has help hundreds of young people in Uganda turn their lives around.

I met adults living in many places of the world that had been raised at Bulamu. Salt Lake City Utah I met a young man named Godfrey. He met an American girl in Uganda and had feel in love. They married and moved to the United States, unfortunately his wife died and now he was raising their young son by himself. Uncle Joseph was a true father to many people and made a huge positive impact on the world. I was more determined than ever to make sure his work continued.

We came up with a plan to put a system in place for Bulamu. Something that can work even after Uncle Joseph, or any of us is long gone. So that it can continue to impact future generations. We would come up with the plan then raise the money later. I had made so many wonderful friends during my adventures in Las Vegas. I knew if we just began the pieces of it all would fall into place.

Kelly's part of the plan was for her to work with 'at risk' teenagers in Las Vegas. After all that is a part of giving back to young people as well. We are all connected in the world after all. The reason she decided to take up the cause was because she wished someone had been in her life to guide her during that time.

Kelly is an introverted person, unlike me. However, if you look at her style of dress, you will know is she is a lot of fun. Bright colored outfits against her fair skin, her hair color changes with each trip to the salon. This month she might be feeling blue, next pink and then purple the next. Nevertheless, she values her alone time. I respect that.

After having Covid, I moved in with Kelly in her apartment. That way we would both have the support of a friend, share the expenses. We got to be two single ladies living 2 and a half miles from the famous Las Vegas strip. The goal that I had with Barb just two years earlier was finally coming true. I had my fun single life close to the famous Las Vegas strip and we had a plan in place to grow Mother Martha Family Foundation.

Sam and I remained in touch and became close friends. When his wife Brenda went into labor with their son Brandon, he called me in Las Vegas. I understood he was a first-time father, and he was calling his friend that is a nurse because he was a nervous first-time father. It was a blessing to welcome Brandon into the world from 10,000 miles away. He had his loving family plus an American Auntie that could not wait to "hug the bananas out of him" when I got back to Uganda.

My friend Daniel that had taken pictures for me in Uganda, we spoke frequently. There is a 10-hour time difference and we both work wild work schedules. Daniel had become a member of my family.

Daniel called me from Kampala while on a roof top above the violence at the end of 2020. He is a film maker, so he just filmed what he saw below him. The next day the newspapers in Uganda reported 203 deaths that day. The reason for the increased violence was because Bobi Wine the leader of the People Power movement, was running for President against the dictator. Mr., Wine had won the hearts of the people of Uganda. He was prevailing over the man that had suppressed the country of Uganda for 34 years. Like every dictator before him, he was not going to just step down. Even if that meant he caused the streets to become bloody.

It is all incredibly sad for the people of Uganda and for humanity. The entire time I was concerned about the children not just at Bulamu but for the 2.5 million orphans that were on the streets. With the violence in the streets, I was concerned about how many more orphans there would be due to the violence. already had now there were more orphans. The goal that I had set to help the children of Bulamu had become a bigger challenge.

I prayed for my friend Zaake Francis daily. I felt a strong connection to the country of Uganda and the people. Something that began with my connection to Geofrey in 2014.

My story did not end with me running off with a great love or a Prince. But I guess I had found a great love. The love and passion I had to help the children in Uganda, and through Kelly's work with the youth of Las Vegas. Now the violence in Uganda began to clear, and the country was beginning its renewal. Just like I went through mine that last few years. I was waiting to take that journey across the globe to Uganda once again to see my family.

I miss 'my twin' John every day. Even though we talk almost every day, it was not the same as being able to hug him and look him in the face. Excitement filled my heart every time I think about Sam driving me through the streets of Kampala. I miss being a Bulamu with Catherine, we have a special bond. I look forward to more adventures in Uganda with all my family there.

Just a few years before I had left my home in West Virginia a broken, abused woman owning just a suitcase full of a few personal items. When I sat on the bench next to the black grand piano at Minneapolis Saint Paul Airport, I was a shell of a person.

I moved across the country to one of the most iconic cities in the world, Las Vegas, Nevada. I traveled 10,000 miles to the other side of the planet. I saw all the sights I always wanted to see. I started to form a new family in the place of everything I had lost. I had a new passion in my life to help children. I learned who I was truly was underneath all the things people told me that I was, I was, indeed, none of the things other people told me that I was. I was strong, wise, sassy, humorous, and I have great style. Greatest thing I found out was that I was loved.

That, my friends, is how a nurse from West Virginia becomes known as "Mother Martha" in the east African country of Uganda.

Made in United States
Orlando, FL
02 October 2022